inspiration
from the
Ellerslie
Flower Show

*Hilary from David & Annette
October 2008*

To all those volunteers, growers, artists and designers who
each year build the Ellerslie Flower Show from nothing;
they live it, breathe it, and keep coming back for more.

First published in 2004
by New Holland Publishers (NZ) Ltd
Auckland • Sydney • London • Cape Town

218 Lake Road, Northcote
Auckland, New Zealand

14 Aquatic Drive, Frenchs Forest
NSW 2086, Australia

86–88 Edgware Road, London W2 2EA
United Kingdom

80 McKenzie Street, Cape Town 8001
South Africa

www.newhollandpublishers.co.nz

Copyright © 2004 in text: Neil Ross
Copyright © 2004 in photography: Gil Hanly
except where otherwise specified (see page 159)
Copyright © 2004 New Holland Publishers (NZ) Ltd

ISBN-13: 978 1 86966 061 1
ISBN-10: 1 86966 061 7

Managing editor: Matt Turner
Design: Gina Hochstein
Editor: Kate Stone
Comissioned by Renée Lang

A catalogue record for this book is available
from the National Library of New Zealand

2 4 6 8 10 9 7 5 3

Colour reproduction by Pica Digital Pte Ltd,
Singapore

Printed in China through Phoenix Offset,
Hong Kong

inspiration
from the
Ellerslie
Flower Show

Neil Ross and Gil Hanly

NH
NEW
HOLLAND

Asplenium
bulbiferum

Contents

Foreword

It's the 'Big Day Out' for the green-fingered. Since that first show back in November 1994, the Ellerslie Flower Show has been the major highlight on the New Zealand gardening calendar.

Around 70,000 visitors annually make the pilgrimage to the Manurewa Regional Botanic Gardens for the pleasure and privilege of seeing the best Kiwi gardening has to offer. The mildly interested are there alongside the devout gardening cognoscenti, and — to the eternal credit of the organisers — there's always enough variety to tantalise all tastes and styles.

Since its debut Ellerslie has gained a well-deserved reputation for innovation and for being a champion of good old-fashioned design excellence and beautifully presented plants. The exhibits might have only existed for a few days, but the well-chosen images in this book are a permanent reminder of their fleeting charms.

The New Zealand gardening scene is lucky to have Gil Hanly. More than any other single photographer she has captured most of our finest gardens and proudest horticultural moments. As a keen gardener herself, Gil is genuinely interested in her subject matter and in a career spanning more than 20 years she has retained her dedication and enthusiasm for her craft.

Gil has been to every single Ellerslie Flower Show and shot thousands of rolls of film. Her indefatigable, all-seeing eye is always there to catch the early morning or evening light, tirelessly repositioning to get the best angle on the design and the plants.

You can relax in the knowledge that the photographs selected for this book are a fair representation of the crème de la crème of every year that the Show has been running.

Neil Ross brings the full range of his not inconsiderable skills to this book project. As a former gardener at Sissinghurst, in the United Kingdom, and Ayrlies here in New Zealand, he has true hands-on experience of what it takes to sustain a magnificent garden of world repute.

His involvement with Beverley McConnell's award-winning Ayrlies' exhibit at the Ellerslie Flower Show makes him ideally placed to write about the 'full monty' of the flower show experience and all it has to offer. He is also one of that rare breed of gardeners who can write with effortless familiarity and humour about their passion.

Now, more than a decade on, the Ellerslie Flower Show remains at heart a wholesome celebration of gardening and a great day out.

If you've ever harboured a thought of going to just one flower show in your life, if only to see for yourself what all the fuss was about, then the Ellerslie Flower Show is your one-stop shop in New Zealand.

As a lasting memento of the Show's fine history, this book is probably all you need.

Maggie Barry

Introduction

When the Ellerslie Flower Show first opened its doors there was little doubt that New Zealand was ready for a national gardening event. Such was the enthusiasm of people falling over themselves to get there that on the morning of 17 November 1994 the infrastructure of central Auckland ground to a dramatic halt as people headed to the Ellerslie racecourse like bees to a hive of honey. New Zealanders hate to queue so everyone had hit upon the same brilliant idea — turn up early.

Twenty tour buses arrived in the first hour alone. By early morning 20,000 keen visitors (some carried down the underpass stairs in their wheelchairs) had shoehorned themselves through the narrow tunnel under the Ellerslie racetrack to sample the delights on offer within. The single huge marquee in the centre bulged at the seams, the dry grass paths turned to dust and those hopeful of avoiding the queues found themselves queuing for everything. The Ellerslie Flower Show had arrived with a bang. For the Rotary Club of

LEFT AND ABOVE: Show icons: The giant flower pot, used by many as a meeting place, and Alison Lennox's trellis trompe-l'oeil *design are recognisable symbols of the show.*

Auckland back then, with its army of volunteers, it was a steep learning curve. But the Show has now moved beyond those first teething problems to become the largest flower and garden show in the Southern Hemisphere.

So much skill, imagination and passion are poured into the Ellerslie gardens that it seems fitting to preserve at least a little of that magic in the form of this book.

The idea for a flower show began early in 1993 when the Rotary Club of Auckland was looking for a major fundraising event that would contribute to its many charitable and community projects. John Anderson mooted the idea of a flower show — the biggest and best in New Zealand and something to eventually rival international shows such as the famous Chelsea Flower Show in Britain. It would be a show of not just national but international standing that would bring together New Zealand's diverse garden-related organisations, delight and inspire the general public and raise a substantial sum for charity ($100,000 was raised in the first year alone). The Rotary Club deserves to be congratulated for having had the vision and foresight to mount such a huge project.

Public support meant the Show was instantly on the map as an annual event, but in 1997 the pressing need for a more expansive venue with adequate infrastructure saw the Show suspended for a year while a new home was found and prepared. Thanks to the enthusiasm and hard work of the then Director of Parks Rob Small and of Jack Hobbs, manager of the Auckland Regional Botanic Gardens, a plan was arranged to keep the Ellerslie name but relocate. The Ellerslie Flower Show moved to a site specially tailored to its needs, with roads, flat marquee areas and a landscaped lake at the centre — all set out against a backdrop of native bush at the Botanic Gardens.

Ask people what they enjoy about the Show and you will get answers as varied as the exhibits themselves. There are the flower fondlers and the design gurus out to satisfy their curiosity. There are the armchair gardeners and those who would not know a daffodil from a dandelion, the gadget junkies and those out for a bit of unbridled retail therapy. Whatever their motivations, the flowers and gardens, the artistry and the sheer diversity of the Show work a magic that you can read on everyone's face.

In early November the site is a peaceful green field. Amazingly, in the space of just three weeks something on the scale of a small canvas town is created. Most show gardens take a year of planning. While the organisers run workshops through the year to help exhibitors become familiar with the standards that are expected, nothing can quite prepare them for the hard work and frantic activity ahead in the three weeks before the Show. The typical laid-back Kiwi approach quickly dissolves. Site lines are sprayed onto the paddock, a digger or two cruises past, and soon the site is swarming with trucks, wheelbarrows and palettes of plants. Activity becomes frenetic as the countdown begins; people have been known to bring in spotlights so they can work through the night and even camp at the site in the run up.

The outdoor gardens and the vast Discovery Marquee are begun first, and two weeks before the Show the indoor gardens begin. Every plant pot must be hidden with bark, dead leaves removed, and every piece of pond plastic concealed by the afternoon on the Monday of show week when the judges move in and everyone else, whether finished or not, has to move out.

The breakdown at the end is even more rapid — most gardens have been dismantled within two days, and after a week the dedicated botanic gardens staff move in to rotavate, seed and aerate worn-out lawn and reclaim their gardens for another year.

It is perhaps the fleeting nature of a flower show, and of show gardens in particular, that is part of the wonder — to make something so ephemeral appear as if it has grown and developed over many years. Designers go to great lengths to bring in established trees and weathered garden features, and use clever planting to give a feeling of permanence: you can almost sense them willing us to believe the fantasy, even though it is all over so quickly.

The Ellerslie Flower Show is now the showcase for the best in our horticulture industry, thanks partly to its system of awards and prizes which ensures standards are maintained, if not bettered from year to year. Many top designers cut their teeth and first came into the national spotlight through winning at the Show. As one well-known designer says, 'I owe much of my success to the advice and knowledgeable input of the Show judges. They, more than anything, spurred me on to try even harder — to aim for excellence.'

OPPOSITE: Just five weeks to manufacture paradise from a paddock. Of all the marquees at Ellerslie, the ASB Discovery Marquee is the most eagerly awaited with its giant theme garden within. Here 'Daydreams to Midnight', a flower-filled fantasy, takes shape under a canvas roof the size of a football pitch. Although the 'stone' garden walls are made of polystyrene, designer Karen Lowther makes sure they blend into gateways near the paths made of the real McCoy so that the eagle-eyed public cannot tell the difference. A large pond excavated in the central section sprung a leak just two days before the Show and 3,500 litres of water had to be siphoned out before the hole could be plugged. Although many props, like candelabras and castles, were borrowed from television props departments, on the day it was the 20,000 flowering plants which 'stole the show'. The lure of the flowers proved to be too much for some, however, and one morning Karen was paid the back-handed compliment of being asked to help reach into a flower bed to steal cuttings by a cheeky visitor who was unaware whom she was speaking to.

OPPOSITE TOP: Addicted to the Show: Terry Hatch of Joy Plants returns nearly every year with his tongue-in-cheek exhibits packed full of seriously good plants. This globe-trotting garden features a South African corner where we are reminded how rich wildflower grasslands, crammed with gazanias and rare bulbs, are all too frequently ploughed up for short-term gain.
CENTRE: Where would a flower show be without the flowers? Whether it is twisted trees in a bonsai exhibit, peonies the size of footballs or, here, Dowdeswell delphiniums with a mouth-watering display of show-off spires, we all love to be dazzled by some floral fireworks. Getting plants to look their best at show time, however, takes some cunning horticultural gymnastics and more than a little luck. For every flower you see there are two or more that never make the grade and get left at home.
BOTTOM: Barbara Morris of Redfire Nurseries, who's been involved with every Show since the beginning, probably provides more flowers than anyone else for show gardens. It started when she and some close friends made a garden for the first Show. The result — a sea of flowers carefully blended into a harmonious colour wheel — was a huge hit and people still ring up today for a planting plan. This design a few years later by the same gang (Phil Cook, Bev Cossar and Leslie Harvison) reworks the magic, this time within a crisp, formal framework.

Judging is always an area of contention, and at the Ellerslie Flower Show the unenviable task was led for many years by international judge and flower show veteran Julian Dowle. Using his experience as a judge at the Chelsea Flower Show — the world benchmark in horticultural excellence — Julian encouraged a similar international standard at Ellerslie. A new judging convenor now takes the reins every year, and with a team of over 30 volunteer judges who offer a highly expert representation of the gardening, horticultural and design professions, the high standard of judging has been upheld.

In the early shows only a single gold, silver and bronze award was given to each garden category, but today there is no limit on the number of awards so that every garden that reaches a certain standard is acknowledged. Gardens are judged not just on a crisp finish, imagination and flair, but also on how closely they have followed their original goal, which is displayed at the Show as a 'design brief' at the front of each display.

The public love to discuss and argue with judges' decisions — it's all part of the atmosphere of the Show. Perhaps with gardens more than any other form of art, we all feel we are experts, and the People's Choice Award, introduced in 2002, aims to give early visitors to the show the chance to have their say and to reflect the thoughts of the general public.

Despite the awards, however, most exhibitors would say that it's not the kudos of an award that they enjoy most but the feedback they receive from an appreciative and often awe-inspired public. Manning a garden exhibit is one of the great joys of the Show — yes, there are the same old questions: 'What's that tree called?' or 'Is that plastic or real?', but also there are the gasps and laughter, the wide eyes and ear-to-ear grins that more than repay the effort and creativity that has been poured in by all concerned over the weeks and months beforehand.

The vision for the Ellerslie Flower Show is not confined to entertaining and raising money from visitors to the show: it extends to sharing the joy of gardens with those people who may find it harder to come to a show and to fostering enthusiasm and talent. To this end, each year there is a special opportunity made available for the less mobile to enjoy the show at a reduced price and without the crowds.

The participation of young people has also been fostered through a garden design competition, run nationwide through secondary schools. The Show has raised the profile of horticulture as an attractive career path for creative youngsters with motivation and artistic flair. Some like Ross Bland have thrived under the scheme: his first entry was as a 14-year-old student at Hamilton Boys High School; he won three awards; and after studying landscape architecture, he returned to win another award as a professional designer (see page 146).

The Flemings Student Design competition similarly nurtures young talent. Recent winners have had the chance to travel and compete at the Melbourne Flower Show as part of their prize. With help from initiatives such as these, horticulture in New Zealand is slowly shaking off the misconception that it is a career for older people or for those who cannot find 'a proper job'.

Whether it is designers, stall holders, growers or volunteers, the people who work behind the scenes at the Show do it year after year, not primarily for any recognition or financial reward but for the sense of camaraderie and for the sheer buzz of being part of a national event.

Although judging has kept a strong competitive edge, it never gets in the way of the strong community spirit between exhibitors. Each year in the frantic few days just before the doors open to the public, materials like tools, bark and compost are shared and the spare plants from one garden are used to fill unexpected gaps in another. There are always last-minute emergencies, too. Whatever happens, there are always eager hands to help each other out.

In a fragmented industry the Show has formed a valuable nucleus, bringing together the wide-ranging facets of horticulture into one place where once a year ideas can be exchanged and friendships formed. Designers, growers, floral artists, sculptors — everyone who is involved with plants and gardens gets together. The one thing you can be sure of is that come the end of the Show, when all the plants have been sold off, when every stucco wall and rock has been loaded onto a truck, the mountains of bark scooped up, and ponds drained and folded away, every exhibitor will say they are never going to do it again. Needless to say, though, come the following year, everyone is back for another go.

As well as the small team of full-time staff, the unsung heroes of the Show are among the sizeable army of some 400 volunteers who keep the cogs turning each year at show time. Some are enlisted from local gardening groups, and even the directors of the Show turn out each year to give their time along with all the other helpers.

Beginning at 6.30am, volunteers work in shifts to ferry the elderly to the site, check tickets, manage crowds and pick up litter. The car-park attendants have perhaps the least glamorous but most crucial job. In wet years, just keeping things moving on muddy grass required the skill of a military strategist.

With an event as big as the Ellerslie Flower Show, there are always the inevitable hiccups. Some are small: a cellphone lost in a portaloo or the elderly gentleman who cannot find his car only to remember, after a two-hour search, that he had left it at home that morning and caught a lift in. Some hiccups are more serious: such as the mini cyclone of 1998, which closed the Show a day early because of the damage it wreaked on exhibits and tents. Even the clouds of that year had a silver lining: an exhibitor who had left his stall takings (no small sum of money) casually wrapped in a carrier bag was delighted to find that they had miraculously survived the storm.

We all know that a show garden is not the same as a real garden. Show gardens are more like a piece of theatre; they have to be if they are to stand out in the sea of other exhibits. In being larger than life, however, it is not always possible to be practical. Designers tend to bend the rules, exaggerating ideas and themes and playing them to their extremes. Plants can be in flower all at the same time because we are not going to see them at any other part of the year. Materials do not have to be hard wearing, for they will only be outside for a moment (if at all). Paths can be impossibly narrow because they will never be used; lawns can be minuscule and surrounded with shells or glass beads because the end result will never have to be mown, and a planting can be banked up for dramatic effect because it will only be seen from one or two viewpoints.

Show gardens also do not have to share their lives with those of children, pets and daily domesticity. In a real garden we have to deal with things like rubbish bins and washing lines, how to hide the carport and how to tie the garden in with the house. In a show garden, designers do not have to concern themselves with such prosaic considerations. They can dream without having to be slavishly practical. Although some find this disparity between an artistic show garden and a real garden annoying, show gardens are important in gardening culture. Released from practical concerns, designers are free to be more daring and artistic — to create something out on the edge of what is possible rather than something camped safely within the realms of what is probable. Show gardens are there to challenge us and inspire — to sow seeds that we can take home and adapt for our own gardens, for 'real' gardens.

The event has come a long way, and every year it improves and builds on the progress of the past. In the early years it was the plant growers and breeders who dominated. Today, cutting edge design has come to the fore. The Ellerslie Flower Show will always foster its grass roots relationship with growers, clubs and societies, and seek to present the very best in all areas of horticulture, but in the future the entertainment aspects of the Show will be developed to attract more families and younger people. The role of garden art will likely become more prominent and greater corporate sponsorship may allow designers to create even more ambitious show gardens.

From the good intentions and traffic jams back in 1994, the Show has not just survived, it has prospered, and now ranks as the premier horticultural event in the Southern Hemisphere. It has more than fulfilled the Rotary Club of Auckland's original vision. At the time of publication around $800,000 had been distributed to various charities, and each year up to 70,000 visitors flood in from all over the country and abroad to enjoy a celebration of gardening of world-class excellence.

Inspiration from the Ellerslie Flower Show captures some of the inspiration that designers have shared with visitors over the years, and adds a little practical advice. Nostalgia, national and Pacific identities, fantasy, formality, humour, international styles, flowers and plants, and gardening for small spaces all make an appearance. At the heart of the Show is our love affair with plants and gardens. The Ellerslie Flower Show celebrates that passion and the ingenuity of those New Zealanders, artists, designers, growers and gardeners who know just how best to fan the flames.

OPPOSITE TOP: Fever pitch: eager Show-goers cram into a garden to sniff out what is new and exciting in horticulture. It is easy to shop until you drop, drool over the flowers and admire the clever designs, but you just might have to wait until you get home to your own piece of paradise before you can soak up that other great attribute of gardens — the peace and tranquillity.

CENTRE: Bare and beautiful: cutting edge design is as big a crowd-pleaser as are flowers. The breadth of design at the Show means that within a few metres we can easily find ourselves stepping from a primeval rainforest through a traditional cottage garden and into a parched desert courtyard such as this. The beauty of the Show is that so many diverse ideas come together, all on a scale that we can relate to. Here, Supreme Award for Design Excellence winner Karen Lowther impresses with a shimmering table of water set in an arid-style courtyard for a slick contemporary feel. (Exhibitor: Auckland Regional Botanic Gardens)

BOTTOM: Another great theme of the Show is the celebration of New Zealand plants, materials and artistry. This garden by Mike Pentecost of Christchurch is a typical fusion of rustic and modern inspirations. Rusted iron meets polished aluminium, with Kiwi plants providing a textural supporting act to nicely blur the boundaries.

Harking back

The allure of the familiar is strong. Nostalgic gardens are perhaps the most emotive and personal of design styles because they rely for effect on tickling personal emotions, whether they are childhood memories or perhaps a half-remembered image of a place we may have fallen in love with on a long-ago trip. Even something as subtle as a scent of a flower may be all that is needed to evoke a deeply cherished moment in our lives.

PAGE 16: A family painting of a classic colonial cottage set in a sea of soft perennials was the inspiration for Liz Mackmurdie's country garden. (Exhibitor: Seaview Nurseries)
RIGHT: This cob cottage is typical of the sort built around Sumner near Christchurch by the early settlers. Rex Young built it entirely to scale as a backdrop for his wife's rich tapestry of plants including delphiniums and grasses. (Exhibitor: Willowbridge Perennials)
FAR RIGHT: John Russell and his team celebrate Beatrix Potter's well-loved tales with a walled country garden stuffed full of vegetables, rambling roses and sweet peas. Features from the books, such as the watering can in which Peter hid, the scarecrow made from Peter's clothes and the imposing presence of grumpy Mr McGregor himself all combine to make for a sparkling trip down memory lane. (Exhibitors: Palmers Gardenworld; McGregor's Horticulture)
BOTTOM: Inspired by the styles of two very different Russian painters — one modernistic and one traditional — creators Kathy Dow and Brian Saunders have juxtaposed this romantic foreground against a vibrant, minimalist courtyard beyond the iron screen. (Exhibitor: WINTEC Landscape Students)

They say the grass is greener on the other side of the fence, and that is often how we look back — imagining everything was better back in such and such a year. Part of the attraction of weaving nostalgia into a garden is this same yearning for something we can never quite reach — the allure of the unattainable. When we get nostalgic, it is not the real past that we yearn for; it is more about a manufactured, idealised and sanitised past, rose-tinted, optimistic and sweetened with four sugars. We imagine how it all should have been, not how it was. Maybe it is this optimistic way of looking back that makes nostalgic gardens so cheerful and appealing.

So as we look back for inspiration, artistic licence demands that we be poetic and not a reporter of times past. And as gardens are all about escape, why shouldn't we be allowed to enjoy ourselves and re-invent a bit of history?

My first garden

Most of us remember our first garden. It was most probably the garden of your childhood where you played in the paddling pool with your brothers and sisters on hot days, climbed onto the neighbours' shed roof to pick apples, and annoy the cat, or tended a menagerie of guinea-pigs and rabbits. Sometimes, if you were really keen, you might have been given your very own special corner in which to sow a few snapdragons and discover the magic of that first sunflower reaching for the sky. But more often the magic of the childhood garden is not connected with plants at all — it is about Tonka toys buried in the dirt, water fights, a sister locked in the shed, and

tree-climbing escapades. We might have marvelled at Granddad's vegetable patch for a second, when he took us to pick beans and stuff ourselves with strawberries, but generally the plants were just annoying thickets which, like black holes, swallowed up innumerable toy cars, tennis balls and even the odd pet.

Between this nostalgic vision of our childhood paradise and the present day, fun often gets replaced by good taste and the old childhood certainty that the garden will never change becomes a desire to constantly change everything, to stay fashionable and keep up with the times.

ABOVE: *Geoff and Liz Brunsden always get to the Show before the crowds. They turn up six months early with a sack of seed and a patch of bare ground to prepare these dazzling wildflower meadows. Each year features different 'eye-catchers'. As well as this old shop bicycle, there is a 1952 Ford Prefect car, a flock of concrete sheep and even a topless model riding a lifesize horse! For many, however, the simple charm of the flowers themselves are entertainment enough. (Exhibitor: Wildflower World)*
RIGHT: *Nostalgia junkies get their fix with this fairytale castle drowning in wall-to-wall roses. John Russell has brought to life Oscar Wilde's children's story 'The Selfish Giant'. Every stone of the castle was hand-carved onto polystyrene sheets which were stapled to a plywood frame by Frank Spicer. Only the top metre of the walls were built, so thick were the flowers stacked pot upon pot along the base. (Exhibitor: Palmers Gardenworld)*

The classic Kiwi garden

Many humorous Ellerslie Show gardens take us back to a New Zealand of 30 or 40 years ago. The iconic Kiwi backyard is legendary, not so much for its beauty as for its awfulness. Concrete was the 'it' material of the suburban section back then; indeed the main feature of the Kiwi garden, the driveway, was built entirely from concrete. No garden in the world has a longer drive-way. Running up the enormous front lawn it typically squeezed past the house through the narrowest of gaps, and ended at the furthest reaches of the back lawn at a tiny fibrolite garage.

The undersized garage and the equally inadequate letterbox contrasted with a monstrous 'feature tree', which could be seen from five blocks away. Inevitably it was a either a silver-dollar gum, a grotesque macrocarpa that pushed up the concrete drive with its roots, or an old, busy-lizzie encrusted phoenix palm. Planting elsewhere in the garden was easy because you only needed three plants — each of them in shocking contrast to the other, for example a bloated camellia, a 'Red Robin' photinia and bright yellow exclamation mark of a 'Swane's Golden' cypress. In the backyard things were even less flashy. Wall-to-wall kikuya grass may have been broken up by a lone lemon tree or a row of ladderferns along the corrugated iron fence. This 'tasteful', subdued planting drew attention to the main focal point at the

BELOW: A wildflower meadow adds charm to any garden but takes a little work. Judicious weeding and cutting back is essential, and a rotary hoe every two years ensures that fresh seed will germinate. For the Show, though, gaps have to be plugged by planting individual plants just before opening. (Exhibitor: Wildflower World)

back — the rotary clothesline, which was the centrepiece and the termination of yet more concrete path. While the clothesline was easily big enough to peg out the washing for a football team, it was nearly always empty.

That the prototype 1950s garden is still held dear is evidenced by the surprising number of new designs such as those of Xanthe White on page 26 and the Auckland Unitec Landscape Design Students on page 67 which have taken the retro look, turned it on its head and created something fresh and exciting. By using materials and features taken from the quintessential Kiwi garden, they cause us to reflect and think about what is special about our own garden heritage. It is nostalgia cleverly packaged in shiny new wrapping, but it works.

Storybook journeys

Often nostalgic gardens are not so much based on the past as inspired by the world of fiction — places imagined in the minds of poets and authors and performers. The magic and myth of *The Secret Garden* comes easily to mind. The idea of a magical place forgotten by time with a secret to tell and the hope of a happy ending is a potent blend of tragedy, romance and intrigue woven around the charm of a garden. Most of us know other stories that can evoke this same appeal.

John Russell, working for Palmers, knows more than most how to push our emotional buttons with the stunning designs he has created based on popular children's books.

Mr McGregor's Vegetable Garden is a magical design, where details from several of Beatrix Potter's 'Peter Rabbit' books have been merged and brought to life among the rows of cabbages and flowers of a walled garden. You can see how a garden like this rings people's bells — just the mention of 'walled garden' and we are imagining something beautiful and romantic! Gardens like these not only capture the imagination of older gardeners who have read the books, they also appeal to today's children who can delight in them even without any sense of reminiscing. It is of little surprise that the Mr McGregor garden won the Show's first People's Choice award in 2002.

John Russell's second garden, The Selfish Giant, was equally nostalgic. Based on Oscar Wilde's children's tale about a grumpy giant who was saved from himself by the friendship of children, it included a castle and draw-bridge, a walled garden (again), roses and a wishing well. This was a garden that exuded sentimentality — and the public just lapped it up.

Flower power

Flowers encourage us to wallow in sentimentality. No matter how many designers harp on about form and foliage, there is a hard core of people who cannot resist grabbing the nearest bloom and inhaling its scent. Beyond out-ward good looks, flowers are imbued with romantic associations, with the rose (just ahead of the lily) the acknowledged queen. Not every rose has this power, however. For while the young bucks head for a luscious red hybrid tea, the nostalgia groupies gravitate toward the old-fashioned roses — anything with buckets of scent, flowers stacked like a box full of tissues and a name that sounds old, aristocratic and French. 'Souvenir de Madame Leonie Viennot', a classic climber, is well up there with enviable pulling-power. Then there are 'Étoile de Hollande', 'Fantin-Latour' and 'Claire Jacquier'; 'Monsieur Tillier' stands out as one of the few blokes in this élite sect.

There are a host of other plants which also play on our emotions — irises, hellebores, lavender, peonies, hollyhocks and all manner of other scented flowers. Whether they bring back memories of far-away places, old

OPPOSITE AND BOTTOM: You might wonder why such a sleek courtyard is featured in a chapter about nostalgia. In fact Xanthe White's design takes an affectionate and ironic look at the motifs and materials of the quint-essential Kiwi backyard of the 1960s and '70s, reinventing them to fit the contemporary look. Corrugated iron is reborn as a living wall topped with Astelia chathamica 'Silver Spear' while the beds beneath, rolling like the Kiwi landscape, are carpeted with Pratia angulata, featuring spherical sculptures made from No 8 wire and chicken mesh (BOTTOM RIGHT). Once used by farmers for shelter belts, macrocarpa wood makes a solid decking on which sits 'silver fern' chairs (BOTTOM LEFT). As is often the case at the Show, the apparent simplicity of design belies a mountain of hard work. The nikau palms, for example, proved to be so big that artist Fiona Henderson had to build the paua shell containers around them using a mixture of foam and papier mâché onto which the shells were then glued. Other iconic features from bygone days include a lawn edge made from baked-bean tins (see page 17) and the ubiquitous lemon tree, which here sits proudly in a basket inspired by Maori weaving and made from plastic strapping threaded around a frame. Despite all the familiar materials, this is a garden that feels fresh and exciting. (Exhibitor: Daltons)

Several Show gardens have looked back with a mixture of affection and horror at how we used to garden (or not garden as the case may be!).

BELOW: White edging, car-tyre swans and a gargantuan clothesline could be found in many a quarter-acre section until comparatively recently. (Exhibitor: Pacific Grotech)

OPPOSITE TOP LEFT AND RIGHT: Back in the 1950s and '60s, fearsome fences, concrete and corrugated iron stopped the kids from getting out and next door's wandering willy from getting in. (Exhibitors: Waitako Polytechnic; Pacific Grotech)

OPPOSITE BOTTOM: Lisa Mannion holds back the flowering of her clivia plants for the Show. Here she relies on a good yarn to promote her passion. This parlour is the result: a fictional tale of an Edwardian plant-hunter just returned from the colonies after searching the world for Lisa's precious clivia.

gardens we have loved and lived in, special moments in life or the desire to have lived in simpler times, these evocative plants tug at our emotions as well as our noses and they make our gardens richer for it.

The best place to gather together these romantic flowers is surely the quintessential English country garden. With New Zealand's many European connections, it is not surprising that the notion of the English cottage garden awash with hollyhocks, honeysuckle and elephantine delphiniums has proved to be such an enduring symbol of all that is good about gardens. At the Ellerslie Flower Show many designers have championed the cause of this traditional look.

With fiddly little arches, uneven paths and crooked gates, the romantic cottage garden can hardly be considered a practical style, but in keeping with the Show why not get caught up in some magic? Exuberance, softness, colour and just a hint of chaos, this kind of garden is a celebration of plants and to some (especially those who have lived in Europe) it is more than that, it is redolent of warm sunny days, cricket on the village green and a rich sense of personal memories and heritage. (And, remember, while some people are being transported by flowers and neat lawns, around the corner a Japanese immigrant may be getting all glassy-eyed over a show garden featuring a swirl of moss and some raked pebbles.)

The essence of nostalgia

If it is not done well, a garden that appeals to our sense of nostalgia can seem trite and manipulative. Whatever the clever allusions, the garden still has to look good.

Understatement is often more effective when it comes to nostalgia. When done well, by designers who understand the emotions they are trying to elicit, nostalgic gardens can pull all the emotional strings. How factual or fashionable they are is ultimately irrelevant. They will always be popular; they take us on a journey back through our own lives to some edited highlights and, in so doing, they do what all great gardens do — they reach out and grab us, take us on a journey and tug at something deep within. It is a trip to savour.

Essentially Kiwi

Most of the gardens throughout this book have more than a whiff of New Zealand about them, but some are positively steeped in local colour and culture. It is not that these gardens simply use native plants and classic Kiwi materials, but that they somehow capture and reflect the unique essence of what sets us apart as a nation — our pioneering spirit, our ability to adapt and always our unforgettable landscapes.

PAGE 30: *How often during a long tramp have we dreamt of finding a spa in the depths of the bush? This oasis, designed by Doug and Trish Waugh, combines architectural natives with zesty modern colours, and utilises recycled and sustainable materials such as the iconic iron fence and the ponga log sculpted by Jeff Addison. (Exhibitor: Naturally Native)*

RIGHT: Beyond Chatham Island forget-me-nots, this inviting koru, railway sleeper bench and nikau frond screen emphasise the Kiwi feel. For an authentic dash of detail, Wellington designer Ben Hoyle pinned monarch butterflies around the garden.

OPPOSITE TOP: Confidence counts in good design and Jan Latham's gardens are characteristically larger than life. Planting in bold ribbons of texture suits the gutsy architecture of natives, such as silvery Astelia chathamica *and paddle-leaved puka* (Meryta sinclairii)*. The brazier and nikau palm add just the right touch of 'Flintstones' theatricality.*

OPPOSITE BOTTOM: After gold was first discovered in Otago in 1861, New Zealand saw the last great goldrush to sweep the world. Paul and Margaret Hilton normally grow water lilies in Waihi, but they took a year out to create this snatch of local mining history. An original ore cart looks at home amid the bronze foliage of native grasses, and young kauri 'rickers' are included to suggest the natural regeneration that has occurred since mining stopped. (Exhibitor: Wahi Water Lilies)

Aotearoa is renowned for its diversity of landscape. Gardening, too, is a rich mix of elements where nostalgia, botanical fervour, a bit of humour and pure theatrical fantasy may come together. So it is little wonder that the truly New Zealand garden takes on so many forms and flavours. Often the style is very naturalistic; sometimes it is highly sophisticated and formal; always it is connected to the land — to our flora and landscape.

Recognising our heritage

Asking what makes a truly New Zealand garden is like asking what vegetables do you use to make minestrone soup — you could come up with many answers and they would all be correct.

One reason the true New Zealand style is so hard to pinpoint is that as a people we are as diverse as the islands we inhabit. We did not grow up in isolation like many ancient civilisations, copying, amplifying and refining set styles and tastes; instead we have always enjoyed a dynamic influx of diverse cultures that over time have brought to these shores a wonderful range of tastes and ideas.

As Hugo Baynes, creator of the Pridelands garden in the Dreamscapes chapter, says: 'Because we Kiwis are not steeped in tradition, we tend to travel a lot and are prepared to give things a go. We also tend to be individualists — we borrow and blend our styles and ideas — and it is our willingness to experiment and adapt and not get bogged down in any one tradition that makes our gardens so exciting.'

Unique plants

While an 'English' or 'Mediterranean' garden can be built from a cosmopolitan mix of trees, shrubs and flowers, the New Zealand garden is characterised primarily not by its design or garden features but by its indigenous plants.

Having said this, it is not enough to combine a few natives (a puka and a carex grass, perhaps) to create a 'native garden'. Like any plants, natives can be used well or they can be used badly; the more thought that you give, the more it will show. Natives need to be used with artistry — contrasting textures and leaf sizes and creating areas of darkness and lightness.

Being evergreen and naturally suited to our climate and soils, natives have been inclined to suffer from their 'easy care' label — too often 'low maintenance' is mistaken as 'no maintenance'. They need care and attention, regular feeding and grooming. Adequate maintenance, good design and an understanding of natural plant communities are all essential.

New Zealand's flora is one of the most remarkable to be found on earth. Of our flowering plants alone, three-quarters are found nowhere else. Today we value our unique plants for their wonderful forms, leaf shapes and value to wildlife. But we have been slow to learn. The first settlers — the Polynesian ancestors of the Maori people — valued plants for food, medicine and building materials, but they also burned vast tracts of forest and scrub as part of their hunting efforts. The European settlers who arrived at the beginning of the nineteenth century continued the destruction with saws and axes, stripping the land for its timber. While people from other countries, particularly America, Britain and Australia, collected, cultivated and raved about our incredible flora, we took some time to recognise its worth. Today, thankfully, we embrace and cherish our unique botanical heritage and celebrate it in our gardens. Natives are fashionable as never before.

Capturing the spirit of place

Taking inspiration from the dramatic landscapes of Aotearoa is integral to an essentially New Zealand garden, whether that inspiration comes from the mountains, the bush, the feeling of emptiness on a windswept beach, or a clean clear sky.

Good design is not simply about copying and scaling down some part of the landscape. You cannot plant a strip of native grass and expect it to look or feel like a piece of the majestic tussock-lands of the Mackenzie Country: it will just be a sad shadow of the real thing. Instead, good designers add their own twist on things. They have the knack of distilling and intensifying that seemingly intangible essence or spirit of the original place, so that for a moment, on entering a garden, you are carried away — lost in a forest

OPPOSITE TOP: Designers Trish and Doug Waugh reinvent the traditional knot garden using natives, with Corokia 'Silver Ghost' *hedges outside,* Hebe topiara *inside and native clematis trained on wire diamonds to enliven the walls.*
OPPOSITE BOTTOM: This coastal garden takes us on a journey from the beach through natural plant communities to a backyard courtyard hidden in the trees. You have to imagine the surf but the rest is real — well, almost. Driftwood, seaweed and black sand from the west coast is genuine, but the rocks are hollow replicas. (Exhibitor: Auckland Regional Botanic Gardens)
THIS PAGE BELOW LEFT: Trish and Doug Waugh helped their children paint the bright mural on the walls of this children's playhouse. Naturally Native loves to present indigenous plants in a challenging way. Mossy scleranthus keeps the rain out. The living roof on the playhouse was grown in Tauranga and trucked up to the show in one very heavy piece.
THIS PAGE BELOW RIGHT: Skinny dipping without a care in the world, this reclining bather crafted by Pamela Howard-Smith seems unaware of all the fuss taken to create the forest glade around her. Naomi McCleary had to arrange the craning in of several tonnes of andesite rock from the west coast to make a setting dramatic enough to showcase garden sculptures by local artists. (Exhibitor: Waitakere City Council)

surrounded with the ear-shattering rattle of cicadas and the sweet smell of tea tree or paddling past a driftwood-strewn shoreline.

Ben Hoyle, a young designer from Wellington, believes that our style is typified by its roots being planted firmly in the natural world. The Maori did it first, weaving their myths around the land and its plants. They took strength from motifs like the koru — inspired by the unfolding fern frond to symbolise the spirit of life and growth. Today, although the koru may have become something of a cliché, it is still an iconic and powerful emblem as is the architectural form of the nikau palm which is used widely in sculptures and ceramics.

Nature throws up endless inspirational patterns: from treasures washed up on the beach, to rock formations and the twist in a braided riverbed. The secret is to look closely at what is around you and work out how you can translate those images and shapes into your garden. A simple leaf shape, for example, can be translated into a deck or a lawn or a flower bed. On a smaller scale it might be a simple outline traced in paua shell pieces to decorate a hypertufa seat or it might be a colour that inspires a paint finish for a fence.

Selecting materials

Part of this connection to the natural world is the use of earthy, natural materials, products like tree-fern logs (ponga), pumice, pebbles and shell. From pioneering days come other iconic materials and features no less dramatic or adaptable, such as railway sleepers and corrugated iron.

BELOW LEFT: With a sharp eye for detail and a sensitivity to the atmosphere of the New Zealand bush, it is possible to bring the wilderness to our doorstep. In the ASB Discovery Marquee, what might have taken nature millions of years to sculpt took Trish and Doug Waugh and their team just four weeks for a touch of Show magic.

BELOW RIGHT: Mike Denyer uses every trick in the book to recreate his ideal summer hideaway — Falls Hut, the classic trampers' shelter set deep in the Kaimanawa Mountains. The worn verandah is made from an old fence laid flat, and the realistic, scruffy grass is the natural floor of the show site which was carefully protected under a false floor while the surrounds were constructed. The night before judging, Mike was up late spraying his foreground 'weeds' with hairspray so they held on to their attractive seedheads, and attacking candles with a blowtorch to get a suitably aged look for the hut windowsill.

Although these materials have a certain rusticity and boldness, it does not mean they have to be used in a crude way. As a nation we tend to pride ourselves on our laid-back approach ('She'll be right, mate') and that's certainly part of the New Zealand style, but there is a time and place for occasionally 'tucking in the shirt' and 'getting out of the jandals' mentality. Swanky gardens can still be essentially Kiwi. Our natural resources and our plants can be used in ultra-modern and sophisticated designs, too, which combine the new and the old in a stimulating mix.

Mimicking natural communities

After *The Lord of the Rings* you could be forgiven for being hell-bent on celebrating the grandeur of our countryside in your own quarter acre. There is nothing like a patriotic splurge, but a wheelbarrow full of assorted natives and materials no more makes a New Zealand garden than a pantry full of food makes a cake. Using native plants certainly adds a New Zealand feel to any garden, but to create a stronger sense of atmosphere we first need to be specific about the 'flavour' of the cake we want to make, and then select and measure the ingredients to suit. Looking after your plants is a good start. And combining them in stimulating ways is even better, but having a focused theme will add integrity to a design. When a theme is geographical, such as 'mountain' or 'beach', a garden will have more atmosphere if the plants are carefully chosen to reflect the natural ecosystems found in these places.

New Zealand is diverse so, if you take your inspiration from a specific part of the landscape, your garden will have more focus and feeling. If your theme is bare mountains, weave together low tussocks, alpines and materials which are in keeping (say, an angular scree-like mulch). Rounded beach pebbles and lush foliage in this context would look totally out of place.

Trish Waugh, who with husband Doug was behind all the successful Naturally Native gardens at Ellerslie, feels that being 'site specific' is one of the most important design considerations when choosing plants for a garden. Plants first and foremost have to enjoy your soil and climate to perform well,

ABOVE: Boys never grow out of dinomania. Jon Lambert has chosen trilobite and ammonite fossils for this drought-tolerant garden not only because he has a passion for geology, but also to provide koru shapes with an extra twist. Relicts of the ancient world, these ornaments suit the ghost-like planting of drought survivors including toothed lancewood (Pseudopanax ferox) and the bony fingers of astelia.

PREVIOUS PAGES: Alex Schanzer's elegant stone sculptures thread along a pebble bed, recalling the braided rivers of the South Island.
BELOW AND OPPOSITE RIGHT: Jeff Thomson has fun with that most quintessential of Kiwi leisure craft: the 'tinny'. The lakeside is ideal for the boat-like forms of David Trubridge's 'Bench' perched on the jetty, Don Stodart's seat and, on page 31, James Wright's iron work and Brendon Adam's blue-glass 'SignPosts'.
OPPOSITE FAR RIGHT: Nigel Cameron combines modern sophistication with wilderness, setting a crisp pebble fountain in the reeds. (Exhibitor: Manukau City Council)
OPPOSITE BOTTOM: Weaving together a tapestry of textures, Sandra Arnet depicts the extremes of mountains and forest. Delphiniums and icy blue cedars represent alpine chill while contrasting woven bamboo panels create a pathway to a vibrant subtropical area.

but more than that, out of the cities, where gardens interact with the wider landscape, if a garden is to blend into its surroundings and look rooted, the plants have to look comfortable — almost inevitable.

The Auckland Botanic Gardens, among others, have been a great inspiration in carefully themed planting. Their 'Beach to Backyard' garden is an ingenious journey through several ecosystems. It begins in the surf before heading inland through dunes sewn together with low coprosmas and pingao (*Desmoschoenus spiralis*). Beyond, the vegetation swells around you as wind-stunted pohutukawa give way to deeper forests of rimu and kauri. In the space of a few minutes we are taken on a condensed journey. Each plant has a purpose: telling the story of the shifting ecosystems which eke out a living in their hard fought-for niche.

Harnessing fire and ice

New Zealand is a crazy kedgeree of contrasts — it is what makes it so special. There are places where you can sit burning your bottom in a thermal stream while surrounded by snow-capped peaks! Given this country's amazing combination of alpine ice and volcanic fire, it is only natural that these themes should creep into our gardens.

Terry Hatch was perhaps first to bring the thermal theme to the Show with a garden swirling with native grasses and red-hot bromeliads designed to evoke geothermal mud pools. Tim Feather has also run the temperature gamut starting with a fir garden of flaming sculptures and later sculpting ice caves for his Kubla Khan fantasy featured in the Dreamscapes chapter (see page 68). Most of us, however, will want more subtle ways to represent our thermal heritage. In some ways our barbecue culture reflects our fascination with fire. And even with all the bylaws to keep the air clean and to protect the bush, we still like nothing better than to be in the great outdoors indulging our love affair with the naked flame — poking a charred log, burning a sausage or two and taking in the beauty of our surroundings.

Even barbecues, however, are in danger of being passé. They have become so sophisticated over recent times — like props from a sci-fi movie — that we are turning to a more primeval way of bringing fire into the garden.

ABOVE: To acknowledge the presence of an ancient totara tree in the background of Doug and Trish Waugh's garden, Virginia King added her powerful organic sculptures (see opposite). As Trish says, 'We knew we had got it right when three kuia (Maori women elders) sat in the garden and looked completely at home.' (Exhibitor: Naturally Native)

Today, no self-respecting, fashion-conscious courtyard is without its fire pit or brazier, but, if that is just a bit too rough and ready, you can always invest in the ultimate Kiwi accessory and have an outdoor fireplace complete with chimney built for you.

Recreating dramatic topography

No sooner had the backbone of New Zealand erupted and thrust its way from the ocean than man came slashing and felling the leafy mantle that formed on the surface. Our early destruction of the forests leaves the New Zealand of today a curious Jekyll and Hyde affair, where the ruggedness of the mountains and the dark grandeur of the bush rub shoulders with barebacked farmland taking a smoother roller-coaster ride through the lowlands. For a nation that built its wealth on forestry and farming, we seldom look to these cultivated landscapes for our garden inspiration, even though they are so widespread. Often it takes an overseas visitor to point out how unique this heritage is; bleached brown and beautiful all summer and lit up with lemon candles of poplar trees in autumn.

Our Tolkien-like landscape with its cartoon dips and peaks is testament to the youthfulness, geologically speaking, of the terrain. Wind and rain have not had time to rub down the humps and bumps, and with the native bush burnt off so rudely in places we are left with a raw but beautiful green mantle, ridged and rippled with the passing of countless sheep or the marks of deserted pa sites.

Nigel Cameron is one designer who weaves these forms into much of his work and enjoys the instant drama that such topography brings. His stylised 'molehills' wrapped in turf and set in glistening plains of pebbles are scaled-down versions of the land around us. It may not be practical to mow such a feature, but Cameron's bold designs get us questioning the norm. After all, does a lawn have to be as flat as a pancake? That is why Ellerslie is so much fun: the designs may be outlandish and fantastical at times, but they are not there to be copied exactly; the idea is rather to sow a seed in our imagination and point us toward a brand-new adventure set in our own garden as we become aware of a new angle that we had never even thought of before.

The challenge is to find the landscape which inspires you. It may be the goblin forests on the slopes of Taranaki, shrouded in cloud and dripping in moss; the plump Moeraki boulders perhaps; or a layering of pancake rocks. Whichever one it might be, Peter Jackson did us a great favour with his 'Lord of the Rings' epic — he reminded us once again of how special this country truly is. If Jackson can fit his vision onto a flat cinema screen, surely we too can capture something of the spirit of New Zealand's breathtaking landscapes between the fences of our own backyards.

BELOW: An integral part of the Totara Garden, opposite, Virginia King's recycled totara 'Waka' combines a sense of the past with a contemporary feel.
BOTTOM: Sculpture adds a depth of feeling and meaning to a garden, spiritual, intangible and personal. Peter Collins's blue 'Orbs' add a note of rich sophistication, their fullness contrasting with the emptiness of the grasses below.

Island life

We live in an island paradise bathed in clear waters, but we are not alone. Like a giant blue glove the Pacific Ocean grasps New Zealand confidently and links us to many far-flung islands and atolls. The rich culture of the Pacific peoples who founded our nation, our enviable climate and the caress of the sea itself have given birth to a fresh and unique garden style — one with a confident blend of sunshine, vibrancy and subtropical swagger.

PAGE 46: A colourful lava flow of dancing flowers celebrates the Pacific style. Whangarei florist Amy Boase has stripped gerberas of their petals and painted succulent Echeveria elegans lipstick-red before setting them afloat on puka leaves.

BELOW LEFT: Jenny McLeod's sculptures contrast the rusticity of concrete and wood with the delicacy and luminosity of recycled glass.

BELOW RIGHT: In wanting to create a futuristic meeting space, Nigel Cameron has used symbolic elements like the gateway and fountains to suggest a sense of occasion, while furrowed earth mounds reflect the farmland of the Manukau region. (Exhibitor: Manukau City Council)

New homes

From their island homes the early Polynesians set out, navigating with skill and courage their twin-hulled, ocean-going canoes. Eventually some arrived at the greatest and coldest land mass, which they later named Aotearoa. The adaptations to this chilly and expansive new land were numerous — clothes had to be fashioned from new materials and alternative crops replaced the traditional tropical foods such as taro and banana palms. But the whispers of ancient beliefs, language and customs lived on and evolved into the distinct Maori culture that is celebrated today.

Within 500 years the colonisation was complete and the new arrivals had populated New Zealand from top to toe. People from the Pacific islands continued to come and still they come today — from Samoa, Niue, Tonga and Fiji — joined by many other races, so that today Auckland is the world's largest Polynesian city. It is little wonder, then, that our gardens, as well as every other area of New Zealand life, are strongly flavoured with the richness of island life along with a range of European traditions.

The Europeans introduced gardening to New Zealand — or at least the idea that gardens can be valued as objects of beauty in themselves as well as places in which to grow food — but today colonial notions of garden style are being superseded by Maori and other Pacific Islands influences which are finding a strong and distinct voice in the arena of design. There is a growing awareness and pride in the wider influence and distinctiveness of the Pacific

— its islands, its plants and its people — and flavours from the past are being forged into something new. As Rod Barnett, a professor in landscape design, says: 'We have gone through the forelock-tugging stage to our European ancestry, and now we are out exploring new areas.'

Lush looks

So what defines the look? The Pacific garden is cosmopolitan in nature — like an exotic cocktail it combines strong ingredients and bright colours in a flamboyant fusion designed to make you relax and enjoy.

ABOVE: A detail from Nigel Cameron's garden. By moulding a concrete floor (stained the same cloudy blue as the Firth of Thames) over polystyrene moulds which are later burnt away, Nigel is able to make an enormous circular platform that seems to float in the air. This ceremonial water bowl at the centre is made in the same way. (Exhibitor: Manukau City Council)

Rather than architectural details and busy designs, it is the plants themselves that often carry a design. They, more than anything else, convey the warmth and lushness of an island escape. The key to effective planting is to have confidence in the way you combine textures, form and colours. Boldness is everything — this is easy when you are working with leaves the size of car bonnets, sculptural shapes or streaked and speckled variegations. Such foliage typically takes centre stage, although the flowers that complement them do not exactly walk in the shadows with their strident colours and exotic shapes.

Weaving in natives

What many of us enjoy about the Pacific approach is that it embraces our indigenous flora so well. Whether it is our nikau palm (the most southerly palm in the world), our bold puka or the edginess of flax, the architectural qualities of such plants are valued worldwide. In spite of being strong in form, however, many of our natives are not strong in the area of real flower power, especially come summer once the pohutukawa has done its brief dash. So a marriage with other subtropicals (like blowsy hibiscus and psychedelic bougainvillea, for example) allows for floral fireworks to add another layer and to turn up the heat. It is a fusion that seems to benefit everyone: a perfect blend of the familiarity of home with the seduction of far-away places.

Turbo-charged exuberance

In the Pacific garden, while planting is often quite simple and uncluttered for purposes of easy maintenance, textures and shapes leap out at you at every turn, contributing a feeling of raw energy and unrestrained growth. In today's climate of instant gratification it is this dynamism which is part of the appeal.

With natives and subtropicals you can be enclosed in greenery within a year. The only problem with these turbo-charged plants, however, is when and how to apply the brakes when everything has reached the right size. How often do we find our beloved palm or banana within months rocketing

OPPOSITE TOP: A last-minute paradise. Beginning with a sense of smart formality in the foreground with lines of pebbles and planters, this garden becomes lush with a jungle feel farther back, with palms, taro and a thatched bure in the corner. Asked to create the garden only a few weeks before the Show to decorate an entrance for one of the marquees, designer Tresta Prujean wanted confident colours and sub-tropical planting to provide a resort feel. In the end, the results so impressed the judges that the garden won an award. It impressed the public, too, as they frequently blocked the entrance to the marquee by stopping to admire the planting. (Exhibitor: Palmers)

OPPOSITE BOTTOM AND LEFT: Each year James Wright evolves in his style but always there is a deep sense of the Pacific in his work. The horizontal lines of this copper waka contrast well with the verticals of flax. A diamond tipped-drill is needed to pierce each stone before an iron rod links them together.

LEFT: Easter Island-style heads have become synonymous with the Pacific style, but this gathering was inspired more by James's travels in Africa and the indigenous masks he saw along the way. Each head is made from concrete coloured with oxides and is carved before it fully hardens.

PREVIOUS PAGES: Bruce and Marg Robinson are the Tarzan and Jane behind this 'Touch of Paradise'. They literally made the earth move to create a jungle-like oasis. Show staff watched on nervously as a vast depression was excavated for their watering hole. It took nearly three days to fill from a single hose, and one unlucky volunteer was cajoled into getting in for a swim to disperse the litres of green food colouring which were needed to transform it from muddy brown to a suitably lagoon-like shade. The lush planting shows just how well a cosmopolitan mix of plants can be blended into a surprisingly convincing jungle escape. Agaves, normally from desert regions, look strangely at home beside homegrown plants like astelias and giants such as the old cycad from Japan (Cycas revoluta)*. The backdrop of six gargantuan palms which set the scene had to be delivered to the site on a reinforced truck, along with a two-tonne rock that forms the centrepiece for the naturalistic water feature, which is large enough to walk under in places.*

THESE PAGES: Island style can be simple and chic. The elegant form of this bamboo spiral in Neil Sheat's design helps to lift the eye upwards and out of what is essentially a cramped space. As the major focal point, it is counterbalanced by a mature Phoenix roebelenii *palm on the opposite side of the garden. (Exhibitor: Fine Lawn Ltd)*

out of control in our pint-sized jungles? With careful planting, however, it is possible to have luxuriance and moderation. We can choose the slower-growing palms, for example nikau, and lookalike plants such as cycads, which will give the same feel but will not take over your life.

In today's gardens, where space is often at a real premium, lush foliage can push out the walls by masking boundaries and introducing a feeling of confidence and a sense of surprise, so that even in a small area we do not get to see every corner instantly.

Microclimates

Another advantage of the lush look is that it is well suited to the microclimates of small town gardens where the shade cast by overshadowing buildings, walls and fences can be a particular challenge. In being adapted to a crowded forest environment, many subtropicals will thrive in these shady and dry places; epiphytes like bromeliads have even evolved to take full advantage of nooks and crannies where there is little soil at all, so are perfect where space is at a premium, such as in containers. In shady corners features such as glossy leaves will reflect light and brighten dark spaces, and silvery or variegated foliage will bring highlights where they are most needed.

Scope for experimentation

Pacific is a style that is still finding its feet, but that is just part of the excitement — to succeed outside with a plant we had previously only considered

ABOVE: Using the natural elements of wind, water and fire, Tim Feather has made a stunning contemporary garden. Tim decided to emulate the layered volcanic sands at Rotorua by using roofing material to construct dramatic flame-like screens. Friends and family painstakingly filled the vertical cells with builders' sand, each hand-coloured with earthy oxides. (Exhibitor: Living Earth)

suitable for indoors, for example. Beyond the ubiquitous palm and tree fern, there is a world of exciting plants waiting. In town gardens especially, where houses often afford those crucial few degrees of frost protection, there is plenty of scope for experimentation. And even in the coldest areas, a subtropical feel is entirely achievable if we are creative and determined. We can use hardier material with a tropical look, like some of our natives, or strelitzias and bamboo which look soft but are really hard as nails. Other plants might need a little winter cosseting, such as lifting and potting, or protecting the crowns of dahlias and cannas from the ravages of winter.

Don't desert the desert

Not every garden needs to look like the set of a 'Tarzan' movie. The Pacific style loosely embraces a cosmopolitan mix of habitats which can be blended in any number of ways. If your garden is sun-drenched and exposed, or if you want a more spacious and minimal feel, you might want to take inspiration from more distant shores on the Pacific rim.

In a more sparse and arid look rocks and gravel often play an integral part in creating a spacious and rugged feel. South African plants like aloes, proteas, gazanias and restios create an arid atmosphere, even though these plants enjoy water all year. The muscular architecture of the Mexican desert agaves or doryanthes from the lush forests of Australia will also add suitably stark and dramatic outlines — lit from below perhaps to cast patterns on a feature wall. These plants still constitute 'Pasifika', they still have the essential touch of the tropics, of hot places and plants that are adapted to coastal living, but they create a more spacious and edgy feel. The beauty of the New Zealand climate is that you can throw just about anything together to create unexpected marriages with stunning results.

Blue upon blue

The Pacific Islands are kingdoms saturated with colour and light. The overriding impression is of blue, layered shade upon shade from the inky blue-black of the horizon through to the richness of the ocean to turquoise lagoons and the luminosity of a cloudless sky. Robert Louis Stevenson, when he travelled in this part of the world, wrote of a 'depth upon depth of unimaginable blue'. It is no wonder then that this colour above all others permeates the Pacific garden, whether on a glazed pot, a swimming pool, a frosted glass artwork or the patina on a copper sculpture.

Bringing a feel of the ocean's colours and textures into the garden might involve something as simple as creating a shell path that cuts a relaxed curve through flower beds, setting fragments of paua shell into a hypertufa seat, designing a water feature, a pebble 'beach' or just a fish motif on a glazed pot. All these details will add to the atmosphere and distinctiveness of a garden that has get-away appeal.

BELOW: A potent mix of fire and water, Phillip Luxton's organic stoneware columns provide a show-stealing centrepiece. The fire is fuelled from gas bottles hidden behind the garden, but the inviting circular shapes, the suitably flame-like planting of cabbage trees and cannas, and the earthy colours evoke the feeling of warmth as much as the flames themselves. (Exhibitor: Living Earth)

RIGHT: The fact that gardens are becoming smaller is one reason people are becoming more interested in garden art. It is a way of providing a sense of style and a focal point in a small space. Here a bamboo wigwam holds a scene inspired by the 'sand gardens' we made as children. The spiralling ceramic dish holding water draws the eye down between textural planting of succulents and grasses. Such a Lilliputian landscape shows what is possible even if you have no more room than an apartment balcony.

OPPOSITE TOP AND BOTTOM: The mosaic tradition is an ancient one. It arose independently in many civilisations but not in the Pacific, but that hasn't stopped artists like Meryn Saccente borrowing the technique, however, for her contemporary work. Decorative details such as this help to define a garden's sense of style. Here a pool is lined with a classic tapa cloth design. The four petals appear as reflections of the corrugated iron fountain in the centre, which is shaped as a pod. Coloured pebbles are not common in the North Island of New Zealand, so many of these are imported from Asia.

Strength of colour

In the Pacific garden vibrant colour is celebrated. In our strong light, some would argue that there is little place for the washed-out pastel shades of an English flower garden. Instead, a palette of bright primaries will shout with confidence and balance the use of bold shapes and textures. Strident colours work especially well when there is enough lush, green foliage around to blend the whole together.

The heat of the sun is easily represented in Pacific gardens with hot colours: the brassy yellows of cassias, the burning oranges of strelitzia (the bird-of-paradise flower), or a gash of hot pink from something like a bougainvillea, reminiscent of a coral reef or a south-sea sunset.

The colours of vegetation can be just as stimulating as flowers with outlandish variegations in the satellite dishes of massed bromeliads or the day-glo leaves of iresines and tropical cabbage trees.

With the emphasis on foliage, often the colour in the Pacific garden comes in splashes and bursts and arrives as much from the materials used as from the plants themselves.

Pacific Island peoples love flowers and the custom of using them for personal decoration is widespread, whether it is in a bright garland placed around the neck to welcome visitors or just a single bloom tied into the hair. Floral patterns and motifs are often used on textiles and artwork, recreating outlandish orchids or echoing sweetly scented classics like gardenia, jasmine and frangipani.

Icons and art

Traditionally, sculpture and pots have had a rather conservative place in the conventional garden, but in the Pacific style they have emerged as integral features in the design. So important has garden art become in recent years that it seems almost impossible to imagine a subtropical garden without at least one hypertufa pot spurting water or a koru-shaped sculpture squatting among the taro leaves. Many contemporary garden sculptures are designed for particular settings where their form or rhythm mirrors the surrounding landscape. Often, the materials and the design combine a sense of cultural

identity with nature-inspired motifs and patterns, from the often overplayed koru to the four-petalled flowers seen on tapa cloth. The nikau palm, with its stiff, shuttlecock head, has become another design icon. Jan Latham designs life-size copies in steel, James Wright lets flames spout from the top of his as dramatic braziers (see page 56–57), and James Pickernell has even taken the rotary clothes line and disguised it as a palm.

Whether leaf shapes, fish or Maori motifs, all are brought into play using earthy materials such as stone, ponga, hypertufa, timber and rusted iron. Copper and glass can add a note of sophistication and lightness to these works and, along with the use of flowing water, bring the colour and feel of the ocean back into play.

Colourful accessorising

As well as quieter garden features, it is just as appropriate to reflect the vibrancy of Pacific plants with art work and containers that explode in a rainbow of strident colours. Painted furniture and pots and mosaic work with an intense and luminous zing frequently find a place in the Pacific style. In bird bowls and pools, mosaics can bring an iridescent depth to the water. Tiles add sparkling details to plain walls and bright stepping stones bring a sense of movement and direction across eye-catching expanses of crushed shell. Like the koru, mosaic has become one of the signature notes of Pacific style and is used imaginatively by many designers, from Nigel Cameron who uses it in a very contemporary way, set as detail into bold concrete forms, to Liz Mackmurdie who incorporates it into abstract sculptures bringing a celebratory note to a design.

Rustic or sophisticated?

In the early days, Pacific style was limited to a chunky, rustic look. Predominantly natural materials like crushed shell, weathered timbers and ponga were used to complement strongly architectural planting. All you needed was a truck-load of pebbles, a dash of rustic fencing and an Easter Island head poking out of the palm trees and you instantly had your own bit of 'Pasifika'.

ABOVE: *Julie and Brian Boys explore the development of cultivated food plants with a representation of a Maori food store (left) and traditional stone beds for growing kumara and taro. The vegetable garden in the foreground depicts foods introduced by European settlers. Damon Howard-Smith's pod sculpture in the centre points towards a fruitful future for horticulture in the 21st century.*

Back then the rustic look was not much more than a rough and ready finish. At its best, though, rusticity can bring a genuine earthiness to a garden, but the Pacific style continues to evolve and today, as well as traditional landscaping materials like railway sleepers, ponga and pebbles, there is a highly sophisticated 'urban' look. From polished concrete floors to stainless steel planters, frosted glass and dramatic fibre-optic lighting, 'Pasifika' has gone upmarket. The visual boldness and structural simplicity of subtropical plants seem to work beautifully with these clean, modern designs, but always, no matter how sophisticated, there is still the sense in a Pacific garden of earthiness and a strong connection with nature. That connection might be through the predominance of the plants, the bold use of materials or nature-inspired motifs.

Island time

As well as the look of a subtropical paradise, the best Pacific gardens reflect the very feel and pace of island life. Ever heard of 'island time'? It is that complete lack of urgency that those with a western mentality find so perfect on holiday. Island time is as fluid as the ocean at the front door; the day is casually marked out by the arc of the sun and the shifting tides; seasons change little and the heat can mean that no one is going anywhere fast. The pervading atmosphere is essentially one of relaxation — it is perhaps why New Zealanders are renowned for their laid-back attitude. So in an ever-more frantic and sophisticated world, the Pacific-style garden can become the perfect release-valve, inviting us to slow down for a moment.

As a still-emerging garden style, Pasifika remains hard to put your finger on. Woven into its fabric is a relaxed easiness — sophisticated yet earthy, luxuriant but minimal, the style is as fluid and as wide-ranging as the ocean itself. But whatever form it might take, it is a style that is fresh and distinctive; a style with a confident swagger, which celebrates rather than tolerates our climate, and which reflects our unique position in a water-locked world.

ABOVE: A special fog-emitter fitted to a stone water feature. This bubbling cloud of steam is the perfect way to add a dash of instant atmosphere when space is at a premium — especially if combined with dramatic lighting.
BELOW: Railway sleepers work so well with both New Zealand natives and subtropical plants because their strength and bulk complement the confident, architectural leaf shapes. Our indigenous plants mingle easily with the tropical look — here Kim Macdonald combines tree fern with strappy bromeliads, puka and ornamental taro. The gutsy landscaping, including a drawbridge-style entrance over a tiny stream and the sense of rhythm afforded by the timbers, pulls the whole design together.

Dreamscapes

At some point everyone should put their gardening books away and create a special garden that comes from deep inside them. A garden that is not concerned with being fashionable, or functional or even horticultural for that matter. For some of us, our childhood gardens were like this — playgrounds where we could create out of wood, stone and leaves our wildest imaginings. The problem is that now we are grown up, we have forgotten how to play.

PAGE 64: *Like a colossal old ship moored at the docks, this impressive amphitheatre by Australian designer Jamie Durie creates drama and tension as normally rigid iron takes on a sinuous quality. The water sculpture, incorporating glass tiles, emphasises the fluid feel, and trailing natives like pratia create waves around the inner walls. (Exhibitors: Tourism Tasmania and Victoria; South Australian and Australian Tourist Commissions)*
ABOVE: *International touring troupe Strange Fruit perform a surreal comic opera in the sky.*
BOTTOM: *Kathy Dow's stylised land-scape represents mountains and sea, and while we may not know what the globes represent, does it really matter? They capture the excitement and exuberance of the show. (Exhibitor: Eden Landscapes)*

There is nothing like an event such as the Ellerslie Flower Show for demonstrating what can be possible when the imagination is given free rein. Back home, applying our own expression of an original idea in the garden can bring us an equally satisfying sense of freedom. You may not be the kind of person who wants to dive out of an aeroplane, or tie brightly coloured flowers in your hair for kicks, or display any other attention-grabbing behaviour, but deciding to change the shape of the lawn, or painting the fence red or planting something outside the norm is the type of expression any of us could undertake. The challenge lies not just in coming up with an idea, but in having the courage to do it — to risk making or doing something which others may not like. Gardens that break the mould and challenge our preconceived notions are a raw celebration of our inbuilt need to create. And making mistakes is part of the fun: if you do not like the outcome, it is not as if you have to live with it forever — there's always next year to redecorate.

The great escape

As well as being a playground in which we can experiment and create, much of the pleasure in having an imaginative garden lies in its potential for being a place of escape. Many of the fantasy gardens created for the Ellerslie Flower Show are so wonderfully over the top — so extravagant and implausible even — that they can give us a pleasant sense of amnesia. Like Judy Garland's ruby slippers in *The Wizard of Oz*, as we head out down the steps and outside, the

imaginative garden sweeps us up and carries us away to somewhere else. Whether this is the result of fantastic foliage, psychedelic flowers, roaring waters or outlandish shapes and textures, the difficulties of the day seem to dissolve and for a moment you can almost feel yourself floating — which, in this day and age of highly pressured living, can't be a bad thing.

Bending the rules

Gardening has its roots in the idea that philosophies, beliefs, ideas and dreams can be embodied in a physical environment. What may not be

A DIY attitude and some classic backyard materials result in this stylish garden that is dazzlingly unexpected. A bar-style table sports grass beer mats, and chicken wire, lemons and washing line are reinvented in a design which playfully asks, 'Have we become too fashion-conscious?' (Exhibitors: Skinny Yamamoto, Jarrod Kilner and Meg Kane for Unitec Auckland)

*Samuel Taylor Coleridge's wild poem
'Kubla Khan' is the inspiration for this
daring ASB Discovery Garden. Ambitious
projects like this rely on the generosity of
the horticultural industry and volunteers.
Weeks spent giving talks to polytechnics
and design institutions paid off for
designer Tim Feather, and during the
rapid build-up of four weeks he was
assisted by over 80 willing helpers.
RIGHT: The garden follows the journey
of the sacred river Alph, here represented
by a foaming rill. Along the way, all our
senses are engaged to make the fantasy
become a reality, not just sight but
sound and smell too.
FAR RIGHT: Jenny Pullar uses
dramatic lighting to complement the
planting so that the garden becomes
even more magical as darkness falls.
Fluorescent columns amid black bamboo,
maidenhair fern and an edging of
Helichrysum 'Limelight' suggest
Coleridge's 'sunny spots of greenery'.
OPPOSITE: Midway, the Pleasure Dome
emerges, floating on a sea of flowers
and backed by a curving wall of water
and a glimpse of the ice caves beyond.
Tim felt an over-the-top carpet of
psychedelic blooms suited the trance-like
quality of the poem. Sculptor Kate Lang
hand-carved the polystyrene dome using
interlocking stylised Matisse figures to
evoke the mood of revelling partygoers.
(Exhibitor: ASB Bank)*

acceptable or practical within the confines of the house is often achievable, even desirable, in our outside spaces.

Although chaos is a perfectly valid tangent for a fantasy garden, the more successful designs still tend to follow a few conventional rules such as those of composition and unity in design. A unifying idea or theme will provide a sense of meaning and make it accessible to others.

However, we will always need reasonably level paths on which to walk and places to sit, and plants will probably be important somewhere in the scheme, even if they are used only in a reduced and stylised way.

Once the basic composition has been decided on and put in place, the so-called 'rules' of taste and convention can then be flung out the window — colours can be wild and clashing or muted and sombre. Textures can be rich and dynamic or harmonious and restrained — or anything in between. Even ideas of dimension and space can be challenged by distorting proportions and creating optical illusions.

The world turned upside-down

A show like the Ellerslie event offers a unique opportunity to showcase outlandish and fantastical ideas that may not necessarily be practical in an everyday situation, yet make a good starting point for developing real life scenarios.

Gardens of the imagination are rarely conceived in a vacuum — they often take their inspiration from something out of the real world and then

exaggerate or distort it in some way, either to drive a point home or simply to make us laugh.

The theme of the Unitec students' garden, simply titled No 54, took traditional materials that make up so many Kiwi backyards and then turned them on their respective heads. A washing line with clothes pegs formed a perimeter fence, while grass was reinvented as textural panels on the walls, and was also used for beer mats on a funky bar-style table crafted from stacked corrugated iron. Some visitors to the Show found the whole look just too over the top, but it worked in the most important way in that it got everyone thinking about what goes into the traditional New Zealand garden and how we might use conventional materials in new and exciting ways.

The Discovery Marquee

The Discovery Marquee at the Ellerslie Flower Show, where one giant theme garden is created within, has been a highlight of the show. For four years it was the place where a fantastical theme has been played out on a large canvas. Although the plants are protected from rain and wind, the heat and humidity generated can be a challenging environment for plants. Nonetheless, there is something about the 'tent experience' that heightens the feeling of drama, especially for vistors to the Show. And the big top is the perfect place for a garden with a circus-like ambience, packed with so much theatricality and special effects.

The first Discovery Garden wowed visitors with a journey through time, beginning with the birth of our country with, as its fantastical centrepiece, the recreation of the silica pink and white terraces, a natural treasure that was destroyed by the eruption of Mount Tarawera in 1886. As visitors wandered between prehistoric plants made from foam rubber and exaggerated in size for dramatic effect, they enjoyed smoke machines belching geothermal steam from sulphurous vents built from polysterene by film set designer Kim Jarret. After moving through a rocky grotto and a forest representing present-day New Zealand, visitors were transported into the future by passing

OPPOSITE TOP: 'And mid these dancing rocks at once and ever, it flung up momentarily the sacred river.' At the source of Tim Feather's 'Kubla Khan' garden, water, light and sculpture by Sarah Brill combine to capture the explosive origins of the fictional river Alph before it zigzags toward the Pleasure Dome. (Exhibitor: ASB Bank)

OPPOSITE BOTTOM: Fantasies need not always be wild and tumultuous. Liz Mackmurdie has gathered together soft and sensuous dreams and flashes of brightness to create an imagined 'Moment in Time' — a place to sit and daydream surrounded by soft flowers, the billow of a canvas tent and the arc of a woven willow fence.

LEFT: Hamilton possesses such an eclectic mixture of architectural styles that garden designer Murray Lye has learnt to adapt to any challenge. Here he wanted to have some fun, and use familiar materials in an unfamiliar way. Shade cloth has been sprayed and used for curtains and a dragon tree (Dracaena draco) is framed as a piece of artwork. The part of the garden that draws most comment, however, is the space-age floor. Water-holding gel, usually used in potting compost, has been dyed fluorescent green with food colouring and sealed under perspex tiles.

through a contemporary rock tunnel that depicted the shifting tectonic plates which thrust up from the sea.

When Nigel Cameron was given the Discovery Marquee, he created a vision of an optimistic future paradise using dramatic earthworks, bold concrete walkways lined with lights, and glowing neon sculptures set in gloomy tunnels. But when your design is heading for the clouds you need plants which fit the bill too, and Cameron used suitably punchy subtropicals set against a background of quieter natives. Massed pony-tail palms, their swollen elephant-leg stem bases looking straight out of a 'Dr. Seuss' book, and forests of giant taro standing larger than life, all set against mirror walls, stretched the illusion even further.

With New Zealand's equable climate we are able to grow such an eclectic range of amazing plants — from arid to subtropical — that it is wonderfully easy to throw convention out the door. But just when we think our design is getting outlandish and zany, Nature shows us that she can go one better with a floral freak show which includes the likes of orchids that pretend to be butterflies and bees, arums as black as soot which smell like rotting meat, and streaked and splashed, funnel-topped, armchair-sized bromeliads.

The meat-eaters step out

Hilary Smythe is noted for her exquisitely refined planting schemes, but while on a flight of fancy on the theme of precious metals she hit upon carnivorous pitcher plants from the bogs of North America as her star players, setting them afloat in rafts wrapped in golden gauze. The idea was borrowed from a local nurseryman who grew his stock in polystyrene trays on an outdoor pond. Pitcher plants love wet feet and in nature use their pond-side seat to attract the mosquitoes and flies that provide their food. So in a way, while wonderfully outrageous, the idea was perfectly sensible at the same time — fantastical ecology and off-beat artistry rolled into one.

Hijackings

A plant growing in an unusual way or in an unexpected place always makes for an arresting feature. The often-bright colours and contorted forms of

Jane McIntyre and Watson Grayburn's inspiration for this galactic garden came partly from sci-fi comic books, partly from New Zealand's volcanic landscapes. Lava bubbles up through a giant zipper, and a suspended glass walkway hovers over grasses planted in seismic waves. The peeling aluminium backdrop is designed to remind us that even when we dream, reality keeps breaking in.

succulents, combined with the fact that they can be squeezed into tight spaces, make them irresistible to designers with an eye for a sense of the ridiculous. It seems a little ironic that while cacti at most flower shows are given a straight, corporate image — usually presented formally in pristine pots against clean, black backdrops by rather serious cactus societies and clubs — the succulents are having a ball outside. They clown around on sand-dunes and purple pieces of driftwood, cavort in brightly painted shoes and are set afloat on imaginary seas in bright blue sailing boats. It just goes to show that in the world of escape, some plants get all the fun.

Psychedelic illusions

One of the most ambitious and fantastical gardens seen at the Show has been Tim Feather's Dream Garden, based on the poem 'Kubla Khan' by the English Romantic poet Samuel Taylor Coleridge. Coleridge was reputedly in a drug-induced twilight when he scrawled his vision of a Chinese emperor's ancient dynasty at Xanadu, so Feather had plenty of colourful imagery to draw upon. He set to work with lights and steel, plants and polysterene, water and perspex to conjure up the fantastical journey.

The fantasy begins as the fictional river Alph spurts from the depths of the Earth in a primeval palm forest and snakes on through sunlit fruit-bearing gardens, sweet with the scent of citrus, toward freezing ice-caves (planted with suitably frosty agaves). In the centre, the great Pleasure Dome itself floats in a psychedelic sea of flowers as rich and colourful as a Persian carpet. All around are the sounds of birds, the boom of the poem and the gush of fountains and water jets. The dream garden is pure theatre, and all your senses are immersed in the fantasy. The path carries you along with the winding river to the inevitable conclusion: The 'caverns measureless to man', where between blackened trees and a blood-red neon sculpture the Alph river spirals out of sight through a dark vortex to sink forever in Coleridge's 'lifeless ocean'.

Gardens like these are 'spectaculars', joining the forces of light, space, sculpture and sound to great effect.

There is never a shortage of boats in New Zealand, nor in the gardens at the Ellerslie Flower Show.

ABOVE: Classy echeverias stowed away in Zenith Succulents' lifeboat keep their frilly underskirts high and dry.

LEFT: The Auckland Vegetable and Produce Growers 'sank to new depths' to bring us this undersea adventure, which earned it the Judges' Supreme Award as well as the 2003 People's Choice Award. Above the boat flits a shoal of Florence fennel — with eyes made from Maori potatoes. Almost 1000 lettuce plants were needed for the seabed alone, and many vegetables, like the extra-long asparagus seaweed, were grown especially. While tomatoes make a glistening starfish and onion skins clothe a scaly snapper, somewhere, lurking in an edible cave, a gnarled old horseradish root hams up its role as a crayfish. But no seafaring garden would be complete without a tale of the big one that got away: a man-eating eggplant shark proved just too big for the lead role and never made it to the Show.

PREVIOUS PAGES: A mere 200 million years of New Zealand history under one roof! The first ASB Discovery Marquee offers a journey starting in prehistoric times. Many of the Jurassic plants (based on fossil evidence) are foam models built on wire frames. For this dinosaur swamp, upside-down grass turf makes a suitably peaty pond base, producing just the right smell of rotting vegetation.

The challenge to dream

The concept of a garden being a place where you can enjoy your favourite poem or novel, or an environment in which you can quietly mull over an idea, is not new. Fantasy gardens overtly link the functions of thought and place in the way they play with ideas and push visions. An example of this is a garden that may be empty of plants but contains a number of carefully placed rocks symbolising heaven and earth — a concept that pushes viewers to confront what is elemental in our lives.

Fantasy gardens today are often criticised because they seem too abstract, so far removed from reality. Perhaps we would do well to remember that they are not in any way intended to be fully practical templates for what we might think of doing in our own garden; rather they should be seen as launchpads of ideas, designed to get us thinking in new ways about what is possible. It is too easy to get bogged down in tradition or to slavishly follow the latest trend in gardening.

Dream gardens are important because they give us the chance to break out, shake off our shoes, rattle us out of our comfort zone and move onto something fresh and completely original. So next time you get the chance to visit a 'weird' looking garden, why not stop for a minute and appreciate the fact that someone is having fun. If you stand and look for clues you might begin to appreciate what the creator had in mind and you, too, may even begin to dream.

LEFT: From floral trains to merry-go-rounds, giant chess sets to America's Cup boats, Clinton Bowyer's gardens — which have featured since the Show began — are always fun, and this fire-breathing dragon is no exception. Each of the 5000 camellia leaves which clothe its body are hand-picked, dried, polished and pinned to damp sphagnum moss. Engineering students made sure everything moves, flaps and smokes for an appreciative public, and when the party is over this magnificent beast flies home with a medal round its neck to star in Tauranga's annual street parade.

OPPOSITE PAGE: The idea of one giant, interactive show garden under canvas is unique to Ellerslie. It took eight teams of people just six weeks to construct this amazing slice of New Zealand's natural history for the first ASB Discovery Marquee. We are taken back to a time when New Zealand split from Gondwanaland — when the first plants were starting to colonise the land and the now-extinct pink and white silica terraces of Rotomahana were in their infancy. Here they rise again, thanks to the skilled work of film set designer Kim Jarrett and the talents of Doug and Trish Waugh, Michael Cassidy and Virginia King, among others. From primeval beginnings, visitors are led through a rocky cleft (BOTTOM), representing a more contemporary Kiwi landscape. A cataract plunges from polystyrene cliffs, and the path winds on through bush to exit through a futuristic rock tunnel.

Playing it straight

Strong bone structure and good under-girding are essential to an attractive garden. Without well-defined walls, paths and outdoor living areas, plants would run riot and our outdoor spaces would just leak into one another. Out in the bush chaos is, of course, acceptable, but few of us want unrestrained wilderness tapping at the ranch-sliders. What we need is some well planned, perhaps even sophisticated, order to step out into after a hard day at work.

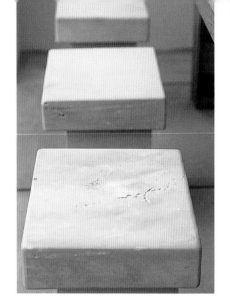

PAGE 80: In this jester's court, instead of the classical tree-lined avenue, ceramic sculptures direct our attention to a more sustainable and easy-care lawn of native grasses. (Exhibitor: Morris & James Pottery and Tile Works)
BELOW: Peter Bazely needed to find 600 identical air plants to illustrate his idea of a garden plant reduced to bare essentials. The elusive stars eventually flew in from California for their ready-made perches.

The beauty of good design is that it acts like a firm circus master — the razor-sharp edge of a path and the uncompromising presence of a stucco wall will crack the whip and pull together the more unruly elements within an ordered framework. Plants, in particular, are like circus animals: charming and exciting, they dazzle us with their party tricks only to run wild when our backs are turned.

Lines through time

A formal garden is reassuring and calming because everything works within a distinct set of rules and nothing is going to leap out at you and ruffle your hair. There are rules of perspective, of repetition and the reassuring predictability of symmetry. It seems that men, in particular, are drawn to the clean-cut feel of formality and its black-and-white parameters. Even before the first gardens, mankind could not resist tinkering with astronomy and geometry — such efforts can still be seen at places like Stonehenge and the great pyramids of Egypt. So it was only natural that the first gardens expressed this fascination with ordering the natural world, and showing off 'man's supremacy' over Nature's chaos.

The earliest gardens were strictly formal. The paradise gardens of Persia, which go back at least to 3500BC, evolved from enclosing and irrigating specific areas, forming courtyards in which a symmetrical arrangement of flowers, trees and water formed an oasis of order and lushness that contrasted with the desert landscape beyond. Each element was rich in symbolism.

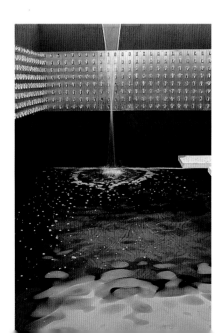

Gardens were split geometrically into four by water channels, each symbolising the four rivers of life which traced the human journey from birth to death. Rows of cypress trees pointed to heaven and, in between these green 'avenues', blocks of lush pomegranate and peach trees, laden with fruit in season, symbolised wealth and plenty. Adopted by Islam and eventually introduced into Europe and western civilisation by the Arabs and to India by the Moguls, these Persian gardens became a blueprint for all the great formal gardens to follow.

OPPOSITE FAR LEFT, LEFT AND BELOW: Repetition can provide a sense of rhythm and order. Here Australian designer Jack Merlo's sophisticated living area shows off careful proportions and clean lines. Succulent Euphorbia trigona *is reflected at the back to add a sense of depth. (Exhibitor: Gardens of Tasmania and Victoria)*

Medieval gardens were cleanly divided too. Paths marked out the pattern instead of water, and raised beds, seats and squares of turf or wildflowers filled in the gaps. The plots were essentially culinary, with carefully tended herbs and fruit trees, but still the layout was orderly. In effect they were the forerunner of today's formal vegetable gardens and potagers, where flowers and food mix together within a strong framework.

Renaissance Europe got hold of the formal idea and threw open the gates of the garden. Instead of looking inward with protective walls, gardens became vast and outward-looking — taking in distant views and stretching into the countryside. The great Italian gardens of the seventeenth century spilled out down terraced hillsides, and in the next century the French took the idea further, especially André Le Notre who laid out perhaps the greatest and largest formal garden: the Palace of Versailles. In these gardens rigid fingers of allées, canals and avenues were planned, radiating out from the house and piercing the landscape in an elaborate show of wealth and confidence.

Orderly to architectural

In the early twentieth century a new style of formal gardening evolved. Replacing the old ideas of symmetry this new formality was asymmetric and minimalist in nature. The new formal gardens were now characterised by bold structure and simplicity in both ornamentation and plants to complement the clean lines of modern architecture which emerged as building materials such as steel and concrete developed.

Today modern formal gardens inherit many of their features from this rich heritage, yet are still happy to borrow ideas from other traditions, such as the simplicity and symbolism of the gardens of the East.

Degrees of formality

The question is: how formal do you want to go? The answer often depends on what sort of person you are and how you live your life. If you are the sort who arranges your gardening tools by size, your wardrobe by colour and your CDs in alphabetical order, then probably you will be someone who works best within a strictly ordered framework and your garden will be no different. Take

OPPOSITE TOP LEFT AND RIGHT: In this 'Blue Garden', fescue grasses are used like specks of colour on a Monet painting to create a shimmering sea of texture and colour. Carefully lit, the water, walls and raked gravel all add to the exciting geometry and come alive in the evening. (Exhibitors: Peter Bazely, Jenny Pullar, Glenice Anderson)

OPPOSITE BOTTOM: Blending a contemporary feel with classic formality, this sophisticated courtyard designed by Anthony Robert Skinner seems perfectly symmetrical at first glance, but interesting changes in the floor levels and textures and a seat hidden in one corner create a pleasing sense of discovery. The loose planting such as the hedge of Buxus 'Green Gem' softens the architectural feel. (Exhibitor: Wairere Nursery)

BELOW: A game of two halves: in 'Green and Grey Spaces', polished steel columns divide the area neatly in two. On one side lush greenery contrasts with the stark, bleached terrace glimpsed beyond. (See also page 92.)

RIGHT: Within a framework of classical symmetry there is always scope to break the rules. In Craig Thorburn's parterre, the obelisks and pavilion have their feet in traditional design but the vibrant paint finish and blue pansies stilt-walking through the marigolds add a playful contemporary twist. (Exhibitor: Auckland Sheltered Workshop)

OPPOSITE PAGE: Leo Jew's crowd-pleaser, the 'Stevenson Garden Zone', is inspired by the New Zealand landscape of beaches and volcanoes. Sky-high purple flower anthers overlook loud stripes of more than 20,000 flowering annuals while over the purple wall, nikau palms tiptoe amongst mounds of tumbled blue glass.

FOLLOWING PAGES: Can a garden be stimulating and relaxing at the same time? In her modernistic design 'Acid Zen', Norma de Langen has combined restful simplicity with colours that go for the jugular. Choosing to highlight the beauty of a few specimens rather than mass planting and cluttering up the carefully calculated sense of space, Norma has balanced lilies with red alcoves opposite, and architectural fig branches link arms across a recess in the back wall. In a garden stripped down to basics, good proportions are essential. Here every element is based on thirds so, for example, the canal is 9m long and 3m wide. The sculptural floor also is split into nine underlit compartments — great for parties, but not so good for the garden owner with muddy boots!

care, however, not to become too much of a slave to tidiness.

At the other extreme some people seem destined to live tornado-style, forever in the eye of a storm — with even the most simple of tasks, like finding car keys, assuming the proportions of a major search-and-rescue mission. Complete informality can leave us floundering in a chaotic jumble.

Thankfully most of us fall somewhere in the middle. We have a relaxed outlook on life but we also enjoy at least some sense of order in our lives and in our gardens, too, to give us a feeling of security and peace.

Getting the look

So what is essential for today's formal look? Formal gardens inevitably look more comfortable flowing from the rigid architecture of the house rather than marooned in a wider garden setting where things can get successively looser and more natural as the garden moves out from the dwelling. The proportions and spaces should relate closely to the house.

Someone who repeats themselves is seen as a crashing bore at social events, but in a garden, when you can't fit in a grand vista or an avenue, you can be repetitive in your design and the result can look instantly stylish and tasteful. Repetition can be our greatest ally in the quest for an ordered look.

ABOVE: The typically asymmetric design in Fiona George's minimalist Japanese garden incorporates unusual materials, such as frosted glass screens suspended by wires, living wall tapestries of mondo grass and a pink canvas sail (see top photograph, page 81). The Japanese approach is to create restful gardens which reflect life's deeper truths. For example, the fact that this light-reflecting pool is partly hidden from view by native oioi rushes reminds us that in life we do not always know what is around the corner. (Exhibitor: Heroic Garden Festival)

RIGHT: Lee Cloke and Helen Boyes have used materials in an innovative way to produce a clean urban feel. The cube seats are made of hypertufa sanded back and sealed with silicon spray for a marble-like finish and the normally flat groundcover Sedum 'Gold Mound' has been grown in tubes of chicken-wire lined with sphagnum moss to produce a quirky slant on the traditional hanging basket idea.

Magnets for the eyes

By introducing focal points our eyes have somewhere to go. In a symmetrical design these focal points might be the highlight at the end of a vista. In a less rigid layout they may simply be surprises or incidents along the way. However they are placed, any features like pots and sculpture need to complement the overall feel you are trying to achieve. A path, and a straight path in particular, acts like a magnet for the eyes — place a pot, seat or piece of sculpture at the end of it and it instantly elevates its importance in the overall design and creates a natural destination.

One of the great things about working with a more formal style is that you can cheat and barely anyone will notice. The power of a straight line is such that it can take your eye and make you forget what lies on either side. So if your plot is crooked, to give it a neatly formal appearance you can divide it up with geometric shapes, lawns, paths or paved areas and be confident that your eyes will feast on the geometry and forget the awkward corners left at the edges.

Minimalism and modern living

Developments in the manufacture and use of modern materials like steel — and especially concrete — early last century led to the rise of modern architecture with its sleek lines and uncluttered forms, and with it came the modernistic garden, where 'less is more'. Presented with a stark wall, a

dribble of water and a stainless steel bench some will applaud the 'courageous simplicity', while others can be heard wondering what happened to the plants.

We now live in times where outdoor living rather than gardening is the priority; where sophistication and ease of maintenance come before a desire for lawns and flowers.

Plant selection

As design has been pared back, so too has our use of plants. Once again, this reflects changes in design and in lifestyle. First, people do not want to clutter

ABOVE: 'Clarity', 'reflection', 'breathe', 'calm' — words rather than plants have inspired this sideways look at how paradise exists not in a place but in the mind. Horticultural student friends Sally McLeay, Jennifer O'Neill-Joyce, Kelly Norris and Glenys Yeoman evoke a sense of serenity, the cerebral elements complemented by black sand for the floor — sourced from a local iron smelters — and planted teucriums.

OPPOSITE: *Surendra Dass likes to think outside the circle. He never doubted that his steel sculptures — looking rather like intergalactic paintbrushes — would provide just the right sense of lift in the pale half of his split-personality garden 'Green and Grey Spaces'. The combination of glass panels, repeated steel rods and columns reflecting the cabbage trees beyond add to the surreal atmosphere and blur the sense of where one space ends and another begins. Much of the garden is constructed from reusable council materials, including street bollards and a giant glass viewing-wall made from unused bus shelters. (Exhibitor: Auckland City Council)*
LEFT: *Different levels always add an extra dimension to the garden, and here a grand staircase emphasises the impressive corkscrew topiary focal point. As in many show gardens, this design by Claudia Daley combines a whiff of classical formality with contemporary touches. Here the garden is partly based on Arthur C Clarke's* 2001: A Space Odyssey, *with cycads capturing a feel of primitive earth, and the monolithic stone wall representing visitors from other planets. (Exhibitors: Hinuera Stone; Standards of Excellence)*

up the simple lines of a good design with too much planting. Secondly, in the past we might have gone overboard with greenery — plants, after all, are a lot more affordable than the hard elements of a design, which might involve some expensive outlay. The result was often a garden mish-mash of impulse buys and gifts along with the risk of some of us becoming slaves to the garden, with practically every weekend spent pruning and clipping, deadheading and sweeping. Is it any wonder that so many of us are turning to a simpler look?

Less is more

Designers today distil and simplify the planting palette, quite often selecting only those plants that are simple to maintain and which possess the clean architectural qualities and year-round good looks which will echo and enhance the strong lines of a well-planned garden.

So often, it boils down to simplicity being the key to success (which can apply just as much to interior design, as many of us know). Using comparatively few elements the minimalist garden relies not just on carefully considered proportions and clever use of space, but top-quality plants, materials and workmanship.

For many people, the formal garden provides order, peace and repose in a fast-moving, busy and stressful world. Whether the design is thousands of years old or an expression of modern design, the formal garden continues to fulfil a vital role in many garden lovers' lives.

A pinch of salt

Are we in danger of become terribly earnest about our gardens? Is the joy of gardening in the process of being hijacked by good taste? With so many magazines and television programmes constantly bombarding us with advice about what fits within the narrow bounds of 'good taste' — as dictated by them — it is easy to get the impression that gardening, too, is becoming all about keeping up with the latest fad.

PAGE 94: *Leo Jew shows that a garden can be both silly and serious at the same time. Taking the idea of 'dining out' literally by setting a banqueting table incongruously in a murky swamp, Leo asks whether the raw beauty of the New Zealand wilderness and our current hunger for sophisticated outdoor living can ever sit happily together. (Exhibitor: LIANZ)*

RIGHT: New Zealand's wire-netting divaricating plants may have evolved to be resistant to browsing moa, but this forest of Yucca elephantipes *could well get pecked to bare stalks by this hungry visitor. (Exhibitor: Sinclair Plants)*

OPPOSITE RIGHT: Often brightly coloured playgrounds can look out of place in a natural setting, but good design is child's play for Manukau City Council, which has come up with this funky tree-house. The rope swings, sandpits and a giant climbing net in natural materials will look perfectly at home when the playground is rebuilt in a local bush reserve after the show.

OPPOSITE BELOW: The lawn reborn. Often considered time-consuming, water-wasting and weed-infested, the Kiwi lawn has suffered from something of a personal image problem in garden design circles of late. This seed company has stepped in to champion the lawn's cause and to show us that even grass can make us grin. Tastefully turfed, this 'Grass Person' irrigates herself after a hot day entertaining the crowds. (Exhibitor: Newton Seeds and Produce)

Are there really right and wrong plants to have in the garden? Are all our cheerful busy lizzies destined for the compost heap in order to clear the decks for fashionable native grasses, some of which are brown and dirty.

And why is the wonderful process of gardening misrepresented as something which is all about endless hard work — lots of frenetic activity with barely a moment to sniff a flower or collapse in a deck-chair with a beer. You cannot read a lifestyle magazine these days without coming across those ubiquitous 'Jobs for the Gardening Month' boxes and being overwhelmed with feelings of guilt.

Humour in the garden

Surely gardening is not just about getting hip and getting exhausted. It may, in part, be a good way to keep fit, and even be something of a fashion parade, but above all it should be a hedonistic playground in which anyone is free to relax and be themselves. Gardening with a sense of humour is all part of self-expression.

Although most of us have forgotten (or possibly not even be aware of it nowadays), humour was once a very important ingredient in putting together a garden. A garden was supposed to be, first and foremost, a place of delight and pleasure. Indeed, the word 'paradise' is derived from the Old Persian word 'pairidaeza', which means 'garden'. Surely paradise has never been a place to fret about the blackspot on the roses and the daisies in the lawn …

Thankfully, New Zealanders still exhibit a pioneering and individualistic spirit. There are many signs that we are still good at doing our own thing and having some serious fun. Sometimes the results are wonderful, like the public toilets at Kawakawa designed by Hundertwasser; sometimes they can be awful; but always it is truly 'us'.

In Europe, to step outside of what is popular or accepted — to swim against the current — is something few dare to try, even in these enlightened times. Here in New Zealand, however, we are not weighed down by those kinds of constraints. In many cases we came to these shores to get away from

ABOVE: Outrageous, plucky and full of character, succulents are prima-donna plants that are made for the stage. Here Michael and Heidi Poulgrain use them to represent crowds on the terraces at a sporting fixture.

all that — an attitude reflected in our eclectic garden styles, with their bright colours, quirky details and innovative design.

Early Renaissance gardens were called 'pleasure grounds'. Back then, the wealthy spent vast sums constructing elaborate stage sets and gimmicks with which to entertain and impress guests. Practical jokes and innuendo were all part and parcel of the great gardens of the time. Water often played a central role with jets and fountains engineered to spring to life when least expected, drenching the unwary. There were fortune-telling mechanical hermits, peasants in costumes and lots of other devices guaranteed to raise a smile.

No self-respecting Renaissance pleasure ground was without its cave-like grotto — with walls encrusted with shells, fossils and precious stones, and peep-holes and passages leading to all kinds of intrigue. And in some cases it was even possible to sail in a model galleon on a specially built canal — and finish off by firing cannon-balls from the galleon into the bushes! In those gardens there was little thought given to form, texture, balance and plant interest: they were all about having fun and games.

Reflections of status and beliefs

In the eighteenth century, before we developed the idea that a garden had to be pretty and naturalistic, the garden was intended to reflect the owner's whole personality — their beliefs, interests and even their politics. The outdoor space was a place to play with ideas and to make jokes through allusions and humorous references. There were all sorts of subtle jokes, such as follies pretending to be real buildings, false perspectives, and *trompe-l'oeils* using mirrors to trick the eye. A statue of Venus might suggest a playful invitation to be seduced; a statue of Bacchus hinted that it was time for a tipple. We think of these features today as being classically beautiful, but in their original playfulness they were not that different from the tinkling cupids of today.

Unfortunately, this long tradition of delighting and surprising visitors appeared to go into hibernation with the dawning of the more serious-minded nineteenth century.

ABOVE: For many, the Ellerslie Flower Show is the perfect excuse for some serious shopping as well as garden viewing. James Pickernell celebrates this with 'Gloria', a shapely example of retail therapy. Carved from a single piece of timber, Gloria's extra-long arms are testament to countless excursions loaded down with bulging carrier bags.
LEFT: Kids often have all the fun. Designer Jill Rice prefers the naturalistic look for her playgrounds and has filled this exciting children's garden with a clutch of interactive features all based on a Kiwi beach theme. An ever-popular rainbow boat is 'moored' off a realistic jetty and board walk. To bring the eternal fascination of water into the garden, Jill has included safe features like a bubbling water stone and a working hand-pump, seen just beyond the boat. (Exhibitor: Enhance Landscapes)

ABOVE: The Wholesale Tree Company's series of ponga passages creates a whimsical garden experience. Part labyrinth, part art gallery, each 'exhibit' within uses a cryptic play on words to celebrate a particular plant and our relationship with it. As a result the mother-in-law's tongue (Sansevieria) is placed forever within earshot (CENTRE), and there are no points for guessing which plant is placed on the plant pot 'lavvy' to freshen the air.

OPPOSITE TOP: Para Matchitt's pierced hearts may seem cupid-like and light-hearted, but they are, in fact, based on a redemption symbol flown on flag pennants by Maori activists fighting to retain their rights during the 1860s Land Wars. (Exhibitor: Waiheke Community Art Gallery)

OPPOSITE BOTTOM: Marti Wong's tool-kit pterodactyl comprises old tools and recycled agricultural machinery welded together. Spot the shovel, fork and hedging shears!

From octopi to Hollywood

Surendra Dass of Auckland City Council continues to blaze a trail at the Show with gardens that bring a smile because they do not take themselves too seriously, with their themes designed to surprise and stimulate. There is the giant octopus surrounded by a psychedelic sea of flowers that rocks to the music of the 1960s. Then came a mystical journey into Wonderland — A Garden for Lewis C. with giants, toadstools and a secret door that might have appealed to that well-known author of children's books. And, more recently, a whole street of grandfather clocks leaning drunkenly against one another to form the backdrop to a carpet of hour-glasses and floral clocks.

Clinton Bowyer, with his team of horticultural students from the Bay of Plenty Polytechnic, is another who is not held back by fashion. He wants us to have fun, and for years he has bent over backwards to make people smile. Clinton's plants, all of them grown by his students, live the life of Hollywood stars. Pansies ride around on merry-go-rounds or giant chess pieces, petunias sail the high seas in America's Cup racing yachts, and camellia leaves become the scales on a smoke-breathing dragon which battles hobbits armed with astelia-leaf swords.

Some of the best jokes are not planned, however. When a model train set launched itself on the scene one year the crowd of transfixed visitors turned out to be more comical than the garden — their heads bobbing like tennis spectators as the little locomotive disappeared into a tunnel at one end of the garden and reappeared at the other.

FOLLOWING PAGES: For the modern couple, Elle Anderson and her team have created the ultimate water feature. Now they can enjoy the great outdoors and still browse the web with this fountain of knowledge. A local farmer grubbing out a shelter-belt supplied the bamboo for the feng shui-based setting. (Exhibitor: Manukau Institute of Technology/Unitec)

A fairy fetish

Fashion followers often get uneasy and shift nervously in their seats when there is mention of giants, fairies and toadstools. It is one thing to have a touch of light-hearted humour in a garden, but small statues with wings, spots and fishing rods? While these themes might be seen as playful or even childish, each of us has a child inside and these themes tend to appeal to that child. Certainly the more wacky and fantastical gardens strike a chord with the public; they seem to get more popular by the year, despite what the gurus of good taste might be muttering in their tastefully minimalist enclaves.

For years the Chelsea Flower Show in London (Britain's premier flower show) banned garden gnomes from the event. Along with brightly coloured figures and fairies, gnomes were considered just too childish and frivolous for such a prestigious event. Gnomes, however, have noble origins. Sir Charles Isham first brought them to Britain from Germany in 1867, and in the nineteenth century it was all the rage for the landed gentry to decorate their rockeries with miniature porcelain figures. Today there has been something of a turnaround. After years of persecution and discrimination, gnomes are making a comeback. Even the Royal Horticultural Society (which runs Chelsea) has relented, and to their credit the gnomes show no signs of bitterness — in fact they are grinning from under their red hats.

Fun should be natural, flowing unforced from the individual's personality. You don't have to be a clown to enjoy a laugh. Gardens are the same — they need not be over the top, or wacky or lewd to exhibit a sense of lightness and wit (not everyone wants to stack up old toilets and plant them with bromeliads or have little cupids peeing into their fish pond). There is plenty of room, too, for more sophisticated and intellectual humour such as the LIANZ garden where a dining table floats preposterously in a pond, making us think about outdoor living and its effect on the natural world.

The vanishing see-saw

There is one type of garden where even the straight-laced agree that humour is not only allowable but essential, and that is in children's gardens. Just why

OPPOSITE TOP: Several of plantsman Terry Hatch's gardens feature himself with the grandchildren. Here, it is time for a bedtime story in a whimsical garden crammed with interesting plants and details. Terry has had fun with the details like Van Gogh's 'Sunflowers' hanging on the bedroom wall and grandpa's false teeth sitting in a glass beside the four-poster bed, which is spread with Ajuga 'Royalty' and yellow Cenia turbinata. Elsewhere, the bed theme continues: golden plants feature in a sun-bed, aquatics float in an old bath for the waterbed, and in the sick-bed a selection of variegated native cultivars are appropriately breaking out in streaks and spots. (Exhibitor: Joy Plants Nursery. Models by Robin Hill)

OPPOSITE BOTTOM: There is nothing like unadulterated colour to stop us in our tracks and lift our spirits. Auckland City Council has created this vibrant undersea fantasy to celebrate their 'Music in the Park' events. 'The Octopus's Garden' in both sound and psychedelic colour conjures up the exuberant 1960s and the well-known Beatles song of the same title. (Designer Surendra Dass. Octopus by Lunar-Essence.com)

THIS PAGE TOP: Serious gardeners might be horrified at this blatant display of frivolity, but for most of us the 'Sovereign Human Garden' and a gargantuan tap by Debco and Karen Lowther turn on the smiles with a larger-than-life sense of mischief.

it is that only children are allowed to have fun is not always clear, but it is certainly a welcome excuse for some outrageous and exuberant design.

Some local councils still seem a little nervous about creating environments solely for the purpose of having fun, so their playground equipment can be exhaustingly 'educational' and 'instructive'. In our safety-conscious world playgrounds have also become neutered — so safe and sanitised that even the old see-saw is becoming a rarity, considered too great a hazard. Instead of traditional grass, kids now bounce on bark chips, coloured carpet and recycled rubber; and rather than climbing up a tree these days, little Billy is encouraged to wriggle up a brightly coloured pole. But despite this trend there is still much to enjoy in this style of playground garden, and designers using these new parameters are creating wonderful caves and castles, nets and ropes. Not surprisingly, the kids love them — and so would we, given half the chance!

Games

Introducing games into the garden is a good way of showing that you like to have fun, but have not sold out to silliness. A game can be seen as fun packaged up in a civilised wrapper. So the secret is to suggest a sense of fun, but combine it with an air of sophistication.

Features like a private tennis court or a swimming pool are good examples of this, but in today's generally smaller and more modest gardens it will

BELOW LEFT: Surendra Dass reckons he never wants to create something that gets forgotten in two days. There is little chance of that with this fantasy centred on the theme of the fleeting nature of time. This wall of drunken grandfather clocks borders an area of massed carpet-bedding planted with 6000 pansies, marigolds, begonias and carpet dianthus. A giant floral sundial and clock in another part of the garden are features that Surendra has always wanted to try. They are planted with herbs: parsley, sage, rosemary and — of course — thyme. (Exhibitor: Auckland City Council)

BELOW RIGHT: Iconic toy of many a Kiwi childhood, this mammoth Buzzy Bee playhouse does what toys do best — and entertains the young at heart. (Exhibitor: Variety Club — The Children's Charity)

Purple
Piripiri

be more likely that you consider ripping up your high-maintenance lawn and putting in a pétanque pitch instead. Although a pétanque pitch is really just a rectangular patch of gravel or crushed shell, by creating it you are making an essential lifestyle statement. You need not even bother to buy the balls; you can just casually refer to your pétanque pitch and know that friends will instantly be impressed and assume that you are a playful and energetic kind of person — the sort who has people round all the time and who is the life and soul of the neighbourhood. Today's pétanque pitch is the equivalent of that 1980s 'must have' home accessory, the spa pool.

ABOVE: Children's author Lewis Carroll might have dreamed up this magical landscape. The heads are based on land sculptures spotted in Britain. To clothe them thickly with a groundcover of pratia, each was carved out of styrofoam and over-planted eight months before the Show. (Exhibitor: Auckland City Council)

But even the pétanque pitch is now under threat — it is in danger of being ousted by the fire pit as the ultimate outdoor symbol. This glorified hole in the ground perfectly embodies all that is good about New Zealand: a casual outdoor lifestyle that is possible to enjoy for most of the year.

More sophisticated, yet perfect for outdoors, are mind-bending games, such as labyrinths, mazes and giant chess sets. A labyrinth is really just a maze with a single, snaking route to the centre. You do not need acres of land and lots of hedges to create one. These days you can scale things down and form an attractive visual puzzle as part of a terrace or even carve it into a deck. You can trace out the pattern in mosaic, on a bed of shell or white lime chips with mondo grass or liriope 'hedges' between.

An outdoor chess set looks terribly swish as well as intellectual. You might enjoy placing some fancy-looking kings and bishops near the barbecue, for example. Or you could use some quirky alternatives to symbolise the various pieces: carved bits of wood or pebbles, perhaps — even different-sized succulents in pots.

Humour is a wonderfully personal thing — it often pokes its tongue out at those who slavishly follow every rule in fashion. So rather than constantly peering over the fence to discover what the neighbours are up to in their section, try and find humour in doing your own thing — in other words, dance to the beat of your own drum — and see the garden as a playground in which to express yourself.

The last laugh

Even if you still are not convinced that humour has a place in your garden your plants may convince you otherwise. You must have noticed that plants always have the last laugh: why else is it that the ones you like the least are always those which grow the best? And what about that special lily which waits until you are on holiday to flower, or the climbing rose which presents its bare bottom down at eye level and proceeds to explode into bloom up in the eaves. Nature never takes itself too seriously and neither should we, so forget being trendy, forget fitting in: let your hair down and smile — it is only a garden, after all!

OPPOSITE LEFT: The Auckland Vegetable and Produce Growers Society exhibit has become an Ellerslie institution with its incredible edibles honouring popular New Zealanders each year until 2002. This bronze statue of Paul Holmes is crafted from spray-painted cabbage leaves. He spins on a parsley lawn in a sixteenth-century formal garden with a pumpkin sundial on the left, complete with leeks marking time. Other celebrities include TV gardening personalities Prof Walker (OPPOSITE RIGHT) and Ruud Kleinpaste (BELOW), who is seen swatting the notorious fruit-fly which threatens New Zealand's orchard industry. The first celebrity to be honoured was Dame Kiri Te Kanawa (OPPOSITE BELOW) who kept up the smile despite suffering the indignity of having tubes of dry ice inserted under her skirt to keep the lettuces pert and fresh. (Exhibitors: David Farley, Julena Moors, Jim Guthrie)

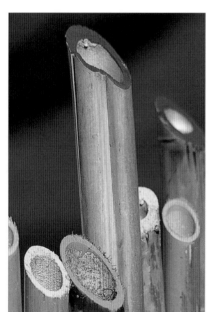

Jet setting

An insatiable appetite for far-flung places is instinctive to most New Zealanders, isolated as we are from the rest of the world. Think how wonderful it would be, though, if you could extend the holiday and somehow bring the experience home to be enjoyed from the comfort of your outdoor armchair. With a bit of imagination and a touch of flair it's not too hard to make it happen in your garden.

PAGE 110: Enigmatic cane sculptures represent Pacific Islands fish baskets or the crane-like water birds of Northern Australia. They emerge from an oily swamp darkened with food colouring for better reflections. (Exhibitors: Jamie Durie for Tourism Tasmania and Victoria; South Australian and Australian Tourist Commissions)
OPPOSITE FAR RIGHT: A rural fruit stall just as you would find in Ecuador.
OPPOSITE RIGHT: In this steaming South American jungle fantasy a toucan watches as missionaries stew in a large pot. (Exhibitor: Plan and Plant)
OPPOSITE BOTTOM: Using authentic species like gazanias and Aloe thraskii, *Hugo Baynes brings an African safari experience to Ellerslie. Lion paw-prints, the sounds of distant roaring and real elephant dung all keep the kids guessing. (Exhibitor: Auckland Zoo)*
BELOW: The lost ruins of an imagined ancient civilisation are brought to life by Auckland City Council.

We all dream of jetting off at some point or other, perhaps to experience a different culture or simply to escape from our everyday lives.

But the homecoming can often be a bittersweet experience, where the pleasure of the familiar mingles with the realisation that come five o'clock every night you will no longer be found propped up at the swimming-pool bar enjoying 'happy hour', but will instead be cooped up in a traffic jam enduring 'rush hour'. Welcome back to the real world!

Imagine, though, if you could extend the holiday and somehow bring the experience home — home sweet home with a happy hour built in! In a garden it can happen, there's endless scope for recreating an aspect or aspects of your favourite holiday environment — it just takes some ingination. So instead of limiting your style ideas to a native garden, a formal or an informal approach, why not go Japanese, Balinese or Cantonese?

Any outdoor place can become an escape, big or small. If you have several distinct parts to your garden (most of us have at least the front/back split), there is the opportunity to try a different theme in each area.

Planning your escape

Small gardens can be particularly well-suited to theme gardens. Because they are bounded by walls and fences they are often inward-looking and self contained — perfect for creating a sense of illusion, and a form of snap-shot with a far-away feel. Glimpsed from a house window, this kind of outlook can become a refreshing view out into a very different world.

A garden with a distinct style always has the edge over a design that is just a collection of plants. Personal memories and inspiration often produce a more authentic sense of a place when recreated in a garden, but if you have not been to Borneo or the high plateaux of Patagonia or any other exotic desitnations you might have to do a bit of homework. Movies, books and magazines are great sources in which to find details of the plants and materials to use, but more importantly they help fire you up and capture something of the flavour of a place.

The search for authenticity need not be too assiduous: it is less important to make a slavish copy than to capture the spirit of a place. A hot desert needs

ABOVE: *The west coast of South America is hot and desert-like and the home of succulents like echeveria and aloes. Richard Davey has constructed a wall of* Echeveria elegans *and a palm-clad hut typical of those used by Chilean workers who harvest sap from wine palms* (Jubaea chilensis) *to make a potent drink. (Exhibitors: Landsendt and Wairere Nurseries)*

to look hot, a lush place needs to feel jungly, and both can be achieved with a wide range of features and plants — in gardening there is always a bit of room for some cheating.

Selecting your materials

A good starting place after deciding on a theme is to remove those features in the garden which are going to spoil the illusion. For example, no matter how much you love that lush camellia bush, you can hardly leave it parked in the middle of your new Arizona desert makeover.

Some plants are discreet — like horticultural chameleons they can fit into a variety of different styles, but some prima donnas are an obvious give-away for a certain look and if misplaced will spoil the illusion. Palms, for example, look strange in a cottage garden, and fruit salad plants (*Monstera*) can hardly sprawl through a delicate Japanese tea garden. It is surprising how just one incongruous plant can completely spoil what you might be trying to achieve. In this respect, it is helpful if any neighbouring features seen over the garden fence work for you, rather than against you. Whilst a large bamboo hedge will lend itself to an Oriental theme, it will be best fenced out or screened if you want to go Mediterranean. In the face of overwhelming opposition — when all your neighbours have gone tropical for instance — it is better to go with the flow rather than try to create a completely different look and hope that everyone ignores the palms peering over the fence.

Your homework will have identified those key ingredients that will act as signposts to announce your intended look. A stone lantern, for example, instantly stamps a garden with 'Made in Japan'. These key 'signpost features' are central to the illusion and you might only need one or two to set the scene. Size is not everything either. It is surprising how even a small detail can speak volumes, from mosaic tiles set into a Moroccan-style fountain to a few seashells left on a table in a seaside garden.

Do not, however, make the mistake of assuming that just a couple of key signpost features will adequately transport you to your chosen destination —

ABOVE: Here these exotic plants are grouped as they would be in their indigenous habitats. Another part of the 'Journey Through South America' (see previous caption) is the impenetrable jungle where Carolyn Melling has used her father's plant-hunting trips as inspiration for a tropical tapestry of bromeliads, many of which originate in this part of the world. The granddad-sized specimen is Alcanteria imperialis. *Hiding under the leaves, frogs and snakes add to the illusion, and, ever obliging, the Auckland weather completed an authentic rainforest feel. (Exhibitors: Landsendt and Wairere Nurseries)*

LEFT: In a jet-setting garden, the hard features and paint finishes as much as the plants have the power to carry us away to far-off shores. In this small courtyard the inclusion of telling details like the brightly coloured poncho and an armadillo provide an unmistakable Mexican flavour. (Exhibitor: Horticom)

one classical statue plonked among your tree ferns no more makes a Renaissance garden than standing in a garage makes you a car. When creating a style you are playing a game and it is important that the whole garden is seen to be playing along with you.

Bending the rules

It is preferable to use the plants which are indigenous to the place we are trying to emulate, but often our climate and the species available in the garden centre will mean that we have to use artistic licence which just adds to the enjoyment. The important thing with cheating is to be familiar with the authentic look you are after in the first place so that your 'stand-in' plants and features will have a smack of credibility.

A good example is Jamie Durie's stunning garden designed to evoke the dry landscape of much of Australia. Jamie plumped for easily available New Zealand counterparts — not just tree ferns but strappy astelias and rushes that would give the look of an arid bush forest. In this garden — like many others — it was as much the hard features such as adobe walls and sculptures as the plants which created the look.

Plants are important, but it is often the design and placement of benches, pots and paint finishes that are so crucial in giving the strong visual clues as to which country we are heading to with that particular design.

Incorporating New Zealand natives is a nice way of blending a feeling of home with the excitement of a far-off theme, and because our flora is

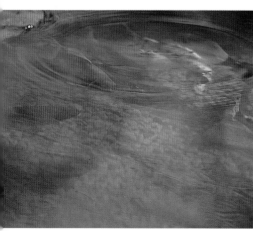

generally subtle in colouration but strong in form, many natives blend into a number of diverse settings. Coprosmas and corokias, for example, will clip easily and can be moulded into highly formal shapes for a classical Italian parterre. Lush natives like pukas and nikau palms make good 'doppelgangers' for truly tropical plants, blending perfectly into a jungle setting. Even New Zealand's divaricating plants with their strange wire-netting foliage have a useful part to play in the jet-setting garden.

Hugo Baynes, when he captured the flavour of Africa in his garden for Auckland Zoo, chose native divaricates, mixing them with brown native grasses for the feel of the thorny scrub of the savannah. Mixed with African aloes, mud paths and thatched huts, the illusion worked a treat and blew the dust off how to use our native flora.

Stucco style

The Mediterranean look is an example of a style many people attempt because it suits our climate (although not always our heavy soils) and it complements the clean uncluttered architecture of many modern houses.

For the tenacious style-seeker there are all manner of classic features with which to pad out the look, from pergolas dripping with grapes, to terracotta oil jars lined up along glaring white plaster terraces, or simple rustic seats nestled between oleanders and jasmine.

In the plant department olives can be a bit over-done, but sweet-smelling citrus and even a palm can make a key style statement. Most spiky, grey or aromatic plants tend to fit into the look, from yuccas to lavender and rosemary! A smattering of colour is also important — perhaps red geraniums in small pots hung on a wall — and plants which are productive like artichokes, figs and vines.

You can also blend in a few suitable natives such as stark astelias, nikau palms and cabbage trees. You may not have a deep red soil nor be able to turn on the 12 months of sunshine, but with the right ingredients blended with style, it is perfectly possible to take a bit of Tuscany to Timaru.

OPPOSITE TOP AND BOTTOM: Although Fiona George's garden has a contemporary slant with photographic murals by Sally Tagg, all the traditional features of a Japanese tea garden are here. (For the Japanese the tea ceremony remains highly ritualised.) The features are simple and rustic with sombre colours and few if any flowers, creating a restful ambience. Fiona sprinkles the stones and plants with water each day as traditionally the fresh glistening look is considered highly beautiful by the Japanese. Washing one's hands in the stone basin is a physical and metaphorical sign of cleansing, after which the visitor crosses mossy stepping stones that invite them to adopt a humble posture, looking down at the feet. At the end of this stylised journey the suitably calmed and humbled visitor must finally get down on bended knee to enter the tea house itself, which customarily has a very small doorway. (Exhibitor: The Japanese Garden Company)

LEFT: The lushness and heat of Singapore are captured by Ben Hoyle with tropical planting around a pergola dripping with orchids which were flown in specially. Oriental screens set against mirrors effectively push out the boundaries, and a table with pebble mosaic forms the centrepiece. (Exhibitors: Singapore Airlines/Tourist Board)

PREVIOUS PAGES AND OPPOSITE
TOP: In Jamie Durie's stunning
Australian bush scene, the muscular
adobe walls are made of rendered straw
bales and provide a strong backdrop to
the planting. Broken as they are with
panels of driftwood and rock-filled
gabion baskets, they make for a textural
feast. The planting is similarly sculptural:
a representation of Australian land-
scapes where rainforests meet the drier
grasslands. Although Jamie used many
New Zealand plants to achieve the feel,
the stand-out stars — spiky doryanthes
and grass trees (Xanthorrhoea australis)
— add an authentic Aussie touch.
(Exhibitors: Tourism Tasmania and
Victoria; South Australian and
Australian Tourist Commissions)
ABOVE: The classical Italian style does
not always sit easily in the New Zealand
landscape, but in the appropriate setting
and with enough marble and ornate
plaster work, why not whisk yourself off
for an Italian adventure? (Exhibitor:
Phoenix Italia)

Turning Japanese

Convincing Japanese gardens are notoriously hard to pull off, not just because the style is so distinct and relies for its effect on a simple palette of plants, but because to be successful you will need to have a feel for the symbolism and philosophy behind each element within the garden.

Japanese gardens are primarily calm and green with brief seasonal bursts of colour — notably from azaleas and cherries in spring and then the autumn colour of maples. Here beauty is not found in symmetry but in crookedness, and those shapes which mimic nature are the most successful. Trees are painstakingly bent, trained and tortured into windswept forms and even the bridges are crooked — zigzagged to shake off evil spirits. Everything in a Japanese garden is symbolic: rocks, trees, water and even the way that gravel is raked may hint at the wider beauty and age of the landscape beyond the garden, reminding us of sea, rivers, mountains and moon.

Some styles are instantly recognisable; others are more obscure. The real test of your success is whether your own theme is successful for you. Does your garden transport you to a faraway place you when you sit out in it? Do you forget the washing and the mortgage and the kids for a minute and imagine yourself in some far-flung corner of paradise? (A glass of wine at this point might help with the image.) Have you succeeded in creating a little piece of an English country garden or a Tuscan hillside complete with figs and olives, the smell of lavender and memories of somewhere faraway but almost within reach?

BELOW: *Forget lush lawns: spiky plants like these* Astelia chathamica, *combined with gravel and bright stucco walls, conjure up a sunny resort feel. With an attractive backdrop, planting need not be cluttered. And as well as providing the ideal getaway, Liz Mackmurdie's easy-care design means you can also take a holiday from the maintenance. (Exhibitor: Wholesale Tree Company)*

Icing on the cake

Flowers are part of life's celebrations and commiserations. In every culture they speak a universal language — tokens that we care. But with the minimalist look becoming evermore popular and all of us looking for easy-care gardens, you might think that flowers are going out of fashion. Not a chance. Their colour, softness and natural exuberance are the icing on the cake — the perfect antithesis to the harshness of walls, paths and paving.

Plants have enjoyed diverse roles within the garden and have not always taken the role of prime importance that many horticulturists insist they should enjoy today. The great Italian gardens relied more on their bold geometry, water and architectural features for effect. In these gardens, hedges and topiary were seen simply as materials to be used to trace out grand patterns. In Oriental gardens, rocks, water and raked gravel were as important as the plants, which were appreciated as much for their symbolic significance as for their looks. Plants in the medieval garden were valued for their medicinal and culinary value, not primarily for their appearance.

It was the Victorians who finally became addicted to the plant world — they filled their gardens with collections scoured from every corner of the globe and they were prodigious breeders of the new and improved. For a time plants ruled the roost and design played second fiddle.

Today's pleasures

Today there is more of a balance. Even so, we are still arguing about whether design or plants are more important in the garden and perhaps we always will. Certainly it was the flowers which came to the fore in early Shows. Ask anyone who visited back then what stood out for them and they will probably remember the flowers: Barbara Morris with her exquisite colour wheel of gentle perennials; the spires on the Dowdeswell Delphiniums stand rocketing to the roof of the tent; and the tranquil lily pond of Wilson's Water Garden.

Plants and flowers are always at the heart of any garden show, and growers and breeders, especially the characters who come every year like Terry Hatch, bring a particular passion — the lifeblood of any good garden show.

Wired to respond

Even if we are not flower enthusiasts, we are all wired to respond to colour. In America, studies of tagging at bus stops suggested that the simple act of planting flowers outside did not just reduce the amount of vandalism: it wiped it out completely.

ABOVE: Karen Lowther creates a graceful 'girlie' garden for a lingerie company by contrasting the softness and exuberance of intense planting with a strongly ordered framework. In the foreground, peonies jostle with other perennials, including the tall maroon spikes of Lysimachia atropurpurea. (Exhibitor: Fayreform)

The red of a stop sign instinctively makes us take notice. Red stops us in our tracks and slaps us in the face — it signals passion and danger at the same time. Conversely, soft pinks and baby blues create opposite sensations: they calm and soothe us, inviting relaxation. The mind-altering way that colour plays with our mood has been used by gardeners over the centuries, and today we are much more experimental and daring with its use than ever before.

Designers now introduce powerful sensations through strongly tinted walls and sculpture. But, although such architectural colour will give an effect for much longer than the fleeting effects of flowers, we still long for the spontaneity and ephemeral charm of a lily bud cracking open or the seductive unwrapping of a rose. There is a certain something about their vulnerability and transience that is hard to resist.

Timing is everything

Karen Lowther is a designer who is never one to hold back with the flowers in her designs. Tulips do not naturally grow well in the warm North Island, so for the Ellerslie Flower Show she grows them in the far south and puts the brakes on their progress with special storage chillers so that they are fooled into flowering two months later than usual. It is attention to detail like this that creates the magic for the visiting public. Peonies, always so popular but similarly shy performers in the warmer parts of New Zealand, are trucked up country in freezer trucks and stored in refrigeration units so that every tight-curled bud is fit to burst on the first day of the show.

Producing an epic

Barbara Morris of Redfire Nurseries is the queen bee of flower growing for the Show. She has exhibited and grown for the event since it began, and has perfected the art of producing fields of soft, sumptuous blooms. These are not the slick architectural plants you see in trendy designer gardens, but cottage-style scented perennials — in fact, just the sort of plants that the public love.

Prima-donna plants, of the size and quality demanded by the Show, need five-star pampering, and each year up to 20,000 potential stars are looked after by Barbara. The taller ones, prone to wind damage, have to be

OPPOSITE FAR LEFT: The perfect place to chill out, reckons Liz Mackmurdie of her retreat. A lime-washed fence blends in with the muted colour scheme and inviting Cape Cod chairs. (Exhibitor: Living Earth)

OPPOSITE LEFT AND BOTTOM: Hilary Smythe had to pillage her own garden for many of the plants in this precious metal-themed oasis. The carnivorous pitcher plants from American swamps catch flies in their funnel-like leaves. They float regally in boats clothed with brass gauze more usually used for filters in food manufacturing. Hemerocallis 'Moroccan Summer' adds the Midas touch, while other features include sluice-like rills and a pool base stepped down in the centre alluding to open-cast gold-mine workings. (Exhibitor: Michael Hill Jeweller)

BELOW: Flowers and foliage work best in combination; here, drifts of tender perennials like marguerite daisies contrast with bold clumps of cannas. (Exhibitor: Seaview/Zealandia)

THESE PAGES: *For the passionate gardener who wants to eat, sleep and breathe plants, Sandra Arnet cleverly redefines the idea of indoor/outdoor flow. As well as a bathroom and a boudoir which features a bed of roses, of course, the kitchen area (RIGHT) is a little more practical, with a barbecue stove and under-bench compost bins, and with herbs and salad vegetables easily to hand around the edge. Sandra has given the garden a 1950s feel with clever use of details like weatherproof cane-style furniture (OPPOSITE) and specially made ceramics. The planting of the lounge breaks normal style conventions, successfully melding soft and colourful cottage garden plants with the architectural shapes of agaves and aloes. Peachy roses include 'Georgie Girl', 'Summer Dream' and 'Pink Abundance', with Petunia 'Sunbells Peach' softening the wall at the front. (Exhibitor: New Zealand Gardener magazine)*

FOLLOWING PAGES: *Sue Linn conjures up a royal red Kiwi Christmas. In this seaside garden, it is the plants, sensitively combined by John Otto, that take centre stage. An exciting fusion of tropicals, succulents and perennials, like the dark Ligularia 'Britt-Marie Crawford', is linked with a thread of larger natives. The colour theme of red and silver ensures that such an eclectic mixture of plants can look like a winning team rather than a bag of liquorice allsorts. (Exhibitor: The Warehouse)*

hand-staked, the mischievous ones that decide to flower too early are constantly manicured to persuade them to continue, and absolutely everything is fed relentlessly; 20,000 plants to hand-water with a secret brew which Barbara will refer to only as 'goo'.

Even in a good year, only about 70 per cent of the entire cast makes it to the final performance: the chance to bloom and appear in an award-winning garden. Some will be sold off to good homes on the last day of the show; those that do not are dusted down and sold on to local garden centres.

Keeping that bloom

Taking a look at the work that goes into creating a garden from scratch for the ASB Discovery Marquee gives you an idea of the extent of the complexity involved. This giant tent is designed to house the largest show garden each and every year. When Karen Lowther was called in to create a flower-filled extravaganza to wow the public, she had just four weeks to clothe an empty space the size of a football pitch with wall-to-wall flowers. Stonemasons and landscapers, planters — and anyone with a helping hand — were called in to create four differently themed cottage gardens entitled Day Dreams to Midnight.

By suspending a giant fan from the tent roof and removing it just before the show, Karen was able to maintain at least some air movement. Powerful lamps compensated for the lack of natural light, helping to keep leaves green, and the actual planting was held off until the very last minute — just five

days before the show — so that the flowers would last the distance. A team of nine women planted from dawn until dusk while 80 helpers recruited from local gardening groups were brought together, working in shifts of 30 at a time, to deadhead, groom, water and fetch and carry every one of the 20,000 perennials that were needed.

The pamperer's arts

In a real garden, you can get away with a broken twig and a spent flower, but for the Ellerslie Flower Show constant grooming is essential, and horticulturist

Louise Reed knows more than most about the intricacies of helping plants deliver an Oscar-winning performance. When you love flowers (and you are after a top award) you want every plant shown off to best advantage, which means constant deadheading and watering, preening and cosseting. Just the trampling of visitors' feet sends up clouds of fine dust each day which can spoil a flower or hide the gloss on a leaf.

The most devoted growers treat their plants like babies and each year Louise is to be found frisking, combing, polishing and generally taking horticultural excellence to its limits. The tools for such fastidious work are found not in a gardener's trug, but in a lady's handbag; for example, nail scissors for trimming leaves, eyeliner brush for removing dirt and dust from the inside of a daylily, and even a surgeon's head lamp for the run up when plants are polished and cosseted well into the night to get everything sparkling in time for judging.

Trees

A character-filled plant like a gnarled old tree instantly adds a feeling of permanence and maturity to a garden, but cannot be bought off the peg from a garden centre. Palms might be easy to dig up but they are heavy and cumbersome to manoeuvre, requiring massive cranes and sturdy trucks to transport them. For the Show, many designers go to great lengths to bring in sizeable specimens to turn on the charm.

OPPOSITE LEFT: With a line-up of white nicotiana, delphiniums and the sunflower 'Valentine', Brooke Stark and her Auckland Botanic Gardens team have turned on the cottage-garden charm with this gold-medal winning potager. It also features a beehive, chamomile lawn and rustic fences draped with sweet peas.
OPPOSITE BELOW: Karen Lowther's epic 'Daydreams to Midnight' display includes a fantasy glade planted with a dreamy mix of foxgloves, ferns and pink Sedum pulchellum. The walls between are polystyrene — blended into real stone near the paths for an authentic look.
BELOW: Around the chamomile seat delphiniums are given the Elton John treatment, with platform heels of hidden buckets to boost their stature. Even little details, like the fallen leaves, took six months of planning — gathered up in wool sacks from a farm the previous autumn and scattered fresh each day of the show. (Exhibitor: ASB Bank)

To exhibit flowers competitively one must negotiate a minefield of rules, regulations and etiquette to avoid a floral faux pas. This selection of arrangements comes from the early years of the Show.

TOP LEFT: Big blooms do not always win points, but these Christmas lilies fancy their chances in a seasonal setting of candles and blue Atlantic cedar foliage.

TOP RIGHT: Heading to the ball. A costume mask nestles up to fantasy chrysanthemums surrounded by delphinium florets.

BELOW: This explosive fantasy is in the ikebana style — the Japanese form of arranging where a very sparse arrangement of blooms represents earth, man and heaven based on a simple triangular composition. True ikebana features only natural materials, but here plastic springs shoot Jacobean lilies (Sprekelia) skywards.

Although many trees are bought or hired from specialist nurseries, some special specimens are dug out of farm paddocks or neighbours' gardens and are returned after the show. When Beverley McConnell recreated part of her Ayrlies garden, she wanted the trunks of swamp cypresses to be a main feature of the exhibit so she took her garden with her. Four hand-picked trees were hand-dug and bagged up a whole two years before the Show, just to allow them time to adjust to their new homes.

Special effects

When Clinton Bowyer's students from the Bay of Plenty Polytechnic needed an impressive cataract of tumbling plants for their dragon garden, they had to suspend plastic crates from a greenhouse roof to allow room for a massed planting of *Dichondra* 'Silver Falls'. Clinton likes to make his plants jump through hoops; when it came to clothing massive chess pieces in pansies a few years earlier, the plants were grown in specially shaped trays laid flat which were clipped together like a three-dimensional jigsaw just before the show. Shade cloth nailed to the inside of the trays held the roots of the plants so they did not all tumble out when assembled in three dimensions.

When plants get together

In New Zealand our equable climate allows for a daunting choice of plant material so we tend to stick to a particular theme, be it Mediterranean, native, tropical, succulent or cottage.

Themed gardens have their strengths and their weaknesses. Native gardens are associated with good foliage and low maintenance, a cottage style means colour and softness but lots of work, and so on. Increasingly, however, we are moving toward a less rigid approach — a fusion of these traditional styles to achieve a balance between the good foliage of easy-care natives, the wow of subtropicals and the charm and exuberance of softer flowers.

In the *New Zealand Gardener* exhibit, Sandra Arnet challenges our pre-conceived notion of garden styles by mixing plants which we would never

BELOW: Although the Dutch are arguably the best growers of cut flowers, our Bay of Plenty is a major player too, producing flowers like gerberas, arums and anthuriums. This asymmetrical massed arrangement is an international line-up, with Cook Island torch lilies at the top, South African proteas, tropical palms and native ferns in between.

ABOVE: A waterfall and river of bedding plants features flowers, flowers and more flowers! (Exhibitor: Peter Titchener; Genesis Training Centre)
ABOVE RIGHT: David Todd creates a low-allergen garden in a relaxed country garden style. The gravel path that winds to a generous cobbled area is wide enough to have fun with some seemingly self-seeding plants. It takes a keen eye to create a harmonious planting like this. (Exhibitor: Auckland Asthma Society)
OPPOSITE: In this easy-flowing and beautifully simple design the architectural qualities of ferns contrast with the strappiness and vibrancy of daylilies (Hemerocallis).
Designer Patrick Corfe likes the way the warm flower colours complement the earthy tones of the ponga trunks and pergola, and the fact that the plants will enjoy the moisture of this cleverly disguised stream. (Exhibitor: Riverview Daylilies)

normally think of together, such as roses with aloes. Similarly in her Fayreform garden, Karen Lowther has successfully blended themes: here a clean, contemporary look complements the delicacy and exuberance of cottage perennials to great effect.

Floral gymnastics

Nowhere is the intrinsic beauty of plants celebrated more at the Ellerslie Flower Show than in the competitive world of floral design. Professional florists and floral art groups from all over the country come together under one roof to compete each year under rigorous international standards. New Zealand is renowned for producing some of the best florists in the world, who have made their name through being adaptable and innovative.

Floral artists are a passionate breed and each year at Ellerslie they work with enthusiasm and keen competitiveness — all except those of the ikebana strand of the craft who are never judged. Their exhibits, inspired by the elements of earth, mankind and sky, are often very simple and deeply symbolic, and like most of the people who exhibit at the show they come simply for the fun of being there and to touch base with like-minded enthusiasts.

A world away from the bunch of brightly coloured flowers we might buy at the petrol station, floral art is a highly skilled discipline combining not just flair but technical expertise, teamwork and no small degree of engineering skill. These days up to 30 per cent of an arrangement can be built of non-plant material, so anthuriums are found spinning in bamboo baskets,

gerberas defy gravity tight-roping along the pelmets of four-poster beds, and longiflorum lilies ride about on coconut boats — it is a far cry from the days when poking a few daffodils into a piece of oasis would do.

Special plants

People come to an event like the Ellerslie Flower Show to be tempted by new releases and unusual plants — to take home something rare and delicious, preferably with an unpronounceable name and a will to live.

Each year certain plants seem to acquire a sort of star status. Sometimes it is an intriguing story which arouses interest, such as the year *Pennantia baylisiana* came to the show. *Pennantia* is a native from the Three Kings Islands and has the impeccable credentials of being the world's rarest tree. Other years it is sheer show-off size that transforms a particular plant into a star, such as the year a spectacular spike of jade-green *Puya chilensis* was on display — people snapped it up, not caring that it can take up to eight years to flower.

In enjoying the gardens at the Show, it is easy to overlook the incredible amount of work that goes on behind the scenes in preparing plants for the event. For example, those bonsai trees displayed in an exhibit at which we glance for perhaps a second or two might well have taken a decade to train and nurture.

But often the 'top-dog' plant comes as a complete surprise — a fifty-to-one outsider that just takes people's fancy. Recently the grass was worn bare round a humble lacecap hydrangea. People gazed, strained to touch and breathe in deeply.

It is touching to see that something as simple and yet as profoundly satisfying as a flowering plant has the power to stop the traffic and make us reach out with that child-like need to touch and even inhale. It just goes to prove that in these days when you can take the caffeine out of coffee, make soap-free soap, even have sugar-free sugar, we should never take the plants out of gardens.

OPPOSITE ABOVE: Eden Garden was created in a former quarry site in Auckland. Director Liz Morrow prides herself on exhibiting on a shoestring — relying on the goodwill of tradespeople and the hard work of Eden Garden volunteers.

OPPOSITE BELOW: Barbara Morris grows many of the flowers for the exhibitors each year — her own dazzling gardens always send visitors scrambling for pencil and paper to take down a name or three. This ethereal cocktail includes old favourites like tobacco plant, snapdragons, delphiniums and a froth of Alchemilla mollis *around the fountain. (Designer: Bev Cossar. Exhibitors: Redfire Nurseries; Phil Cooke; Leslie Harvison; Barbara Myers)*

ABOVE: The bustle of brightly coloured candelabra primulas is almost as intense as that of the crowd beyond as they strain to glimpse this calm lily pond beautifully captured under canvas by Wilsons Water Garden.

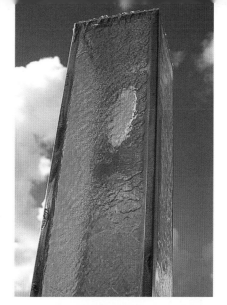

Small spaces

We live in a fashion-conscious world where — whether it is cars, telephones, computers or underwear — 'small is beautiful' is the cry. For gardens it is no different. Boxed in, hedged in or walled in, most of us have at least some part of our outdoor space where we are forced to shoe-horn all our design, ideas, horticultural aspirations, outdoor dining requirements, a shed, rubbish bin and washing line into something the size of a match box.

PAGE 142: Artwork by Dee Melville-Nel is protected by a vibrant shade sail which, along with fountains, creates a vibrant sense of theatre. (Exhibitor: White International)
BELOW LEFT: Jac Spyksma's urban oasis is a shrine to modern living with walls clad in aluminium newsprint printing plates and a floor mulched with roasted coffee. (Exhibitor: Naja Nursery)
BELOW RIGHT: There is a primeval feel to this swirling 'black hole'. Candles and the dark table-setting add a gothic sense of drama. (Exhibitor: Jennifer Russell)

Small beginnings

Small gardens have their own particular problems as well as virtues. Above all there is a wonderfully intimate and safe feel to small places — a private enclave where, with some imagination and care, we can create a space that is both functional and a feast for the eyes.

Small gardens are not just a product of modern urbanisation. The earliest gardeners deliberately chose to limit their boundaries. From the unearthed remains of Pompeii to the palaces of ancient Persia and medieval Europe, early gardens were typically small, enclosed and intimate, a vision of paradise that reflected the need for seclusion and protection from an uncertain world — thoughts which are not that far removed from today's requirements.

Good bones

In the days when most suburban New Zealanders had at least a quarter-acre to play with, the siting of a shed or washing line, and creating room to sit outdoors, was not an issue. However, today clever garden design is essential if we are to juggle the often-conflicting demands on our shrinking spaces.

The first consideration in any small garden is to decide what it is to be used for so that the design that follows is practical. For most of us, having the space to entertain is high on the list of requirements, but there might be secondary issues to consider, such as places to dry washing, store garden tools and rubbish bins, and keep pets.

After making room for practicalities we can get on with the creative side. Choosing a distinct style will lead to the foundation of a simple and unified feel. In show gardens, again and again you will see the repeated use of materials, plants and textures, clearly defined colour themes and either a distinctly formal or informal approach.

In a small space there is never the room to play out all our ideas and tastes — we have to be brutally focused so we do not end up with a garden with not only the proportions of a broom cupboard but also the look of one. In this regard all your features, from sculpture to pots to garden furniture and

ABOVE: Matt McClean's muscular ceramic sculpture echoes the strong architecture of Lord Howe Island palms. The powerful garden lighting takes full advantage of the dramatic shapes and means that this garden could be enjoyed at any time of the day. The cleverly zig-zagged wall at the back is a nice finishing touch. (Designer: Tim Feather. Exhibitor: ASB Bank)

paint finishes, should work as a team in order to reinforce the same feel. As one designer said, 'The most important thing is to have one brilliant idea and to run with it. Everything in the garden should focus attention on that idea or theme or support it in some way.'

Easy care with flair

No longer do we want to mow and prune, sow seeds and hang around at the end of a hose. Today we want to lounge, bask, eat and drink, all in wonderful surroundings that don't involve too much work. In this respect, gardens have changed and today the guiding principles for outdoor living are reduced maintenance and fewer plants. But with all the flesh stripped away, we need to make sure that there is a strong bone structure underneath. The underlying design (paths, patios and walls) has to look well proportioned and appealing, even when stripped bare.

For example, floor surfaces, once overlooked, are now treated almost as pieces of sculpture as well as being places to sit, and many designers combine interesting shapes and materials to give powerful koru or grid patterns which help bind a design together. High-maintenance lawns have been replaced with textural swirls of pebble or glass chippings combined with low-maintenance groundcovers.

The more sophisticated the materials you include — glass, steel, and weatherproof fabrics and canvas, for example — the more the garden will feel like an outdoor room and less like a place simply to peg out the washing. Sandra Arnet, in her Coastal Reef design, chose the exhilarating device of contrasting sophistication with ruggedness for her underwater theme. Pebbles and shells were sealed into a polished resin floor with a watery look that 'lapped' against rugged scoria boulders edging the flower beds.

Heading outside

Indoor/outdoor flow is one of the buzz concepts of modern garden design. By carrying the materials and proportions for floors and walls used inside into the garden, and by removing changes in levels, a link is created between the two areas which can make the garden feel more accessible and attractive.

The development of weatherproof covers is another factor changing the way we use our garden spaces. Even after the ups and downs of the America's Cup, many New Zealanders have firmly embraced a nautical feel in their gardens, with a billowing shade sail (along with the outdoor fireplace) becoming the major garden feature of the twenty-first century. Creaky old umbrellas have had their dash. Unlike the pergola of old, dripping with wisteria and bees, a sail will neither drop leaves on your paving nor let rain and insects land in your soup over dinner. Moreover, it offers not just protection for sun and rain and easy maintenance, but adds instant sophistication.

OPPOSITE LEFT: Jan Latham's clever garden, based on the theme 'Inside out', only reveals its reflected surprises as we interact with the design to catch reflected glimpses through doors and windows. We can spot the sunflower, but a wall-to-ceiling fish tank is still to be discovered. The stylised water staircase and native scleranthus carpet blur the boundary between where the house ends and the garden begins.
OPPOSITE BOTTOM: Designer Heather Mark built this fantasy on a watery theme as a team effort with Natalie Clover and Ross Bland. Heather admits that she was (and still is) going through 'something of an industrial phase', using metal grilles set over blue pebbles to replace the traditional lawn and lead the eye to a steel brazier.
BELOW: For some elegant formality, Hilary Smythe hits an art deco note with vertical rills falling down a sculptural wall. (Exhibitor: Riverview Daylilies)

RIGHT: This punchy courtyard by the Auckland Regional Botanic Gardens is designed to show that edible plants can be incorporated into any garden style. Raised beds make for easy access and the colour-themed planting incorporates not just vegetables but edible flowers like calendula, marigold and nasturtium. Hidden within the elegant walls, a drawer holds 1000 tiger worms which are busily composting garden scraps. But they might well go hungry: in a garden that looks this good, we might never be able to bring ourselves to pulling out the fruits of our labours.

OPPOSITE: Murray Lye has created this optimistic garden with a theme of moving forward into the future. In disappearing into the wall, the man and boy act like a modern-day trompe-l'oeil, *effectively increasing the sense of depth in a small space. The side panels, made from old doors, are set at angles to draw our eye in towards the wall sculpture and to create a sense of mystery. In a real garden the wasted space behind could effectively hide features like air-conditioning units and rubbish bins. The figures themselves were made by sawing up shop mannequins.*

OPPOSITE BOTTOM: Another garden from the Auckland Regional Botanic Gardens team shows a more classical variation on the potager theme. By sticking to smaller salad crops and herbs, the attractive design of paths is not hidden, and composting the waste is shown to be an essential component.

Lighting

New Zealanders love nothing better than to be outside in the evening, and a recent feature that is helping us get out there is garden lighting. Gone are the glowing glass orbs and aluminum UFOs of the 1970s; today's lighting, especially that designed by Jennifer Pullar, is stylish and discreet. You do not need headlight dazzle for impact. Go for quality, not quantity, creating mood with subtle colours and cast shadows.

Whether it is simple spot lights, under-floor effects or neon sculptures, lit gardens look even more stunning and atmospheric by night than they do in the day. Even if we stay indoors with our gardens illuminated and cast into dramatic relief, we can bring a completely new and expanded dimension into our homes.

Boundaries

Softening a boxed-in feel is always a major concern in tight places. Often it is easier to go with the flow and keep a geometric look, but if a confined space is simply part of a larger garden you can have fun punching holes in your boundaries. The Kings Plant Barn garden (page 156) is full of practical ideas for extending the view, with windows and slits cut into stucco walls so that the eye gets glimpses of the wider garden beyond. Even within a confined space, subdividing with a feature wall creates a sense of 'rooms within rooms', as evidenced in Jan Latham's courtyard (page 146), or in Murray Lye's Into the Future garden.

Pigeon-hole planting

Plants are what transform an outdoor room into a garden. A few years ago the trend was wall-to-wall luxuriance with hedges and even small lawns, but today we have stripped down our outdoor space, using interesting textural finishes and hard landscaping. Because the planting is reduced and distilled, each plant has to be a high achiever, looking good year-round. Palms, cycads and evergreen native plants prove themselves again and again, but deciduous shrubs like Japanese maples also introduce a nice touch of seasonality and style, especially if lit from beneath to cast intriguing shadows.

As in the overall design, the key with planting is to use a simple palette of plants for a relaxed, uncluttered look. Choosing foliage for smaller gardens is perhaps more important than flowers, because it is seen all year and, in the tight urban garden, colour can be introduced through many other media, such as pots, sculpture and paint finishes. While injections of artificial colour can look contrived in a rambling country garden, in cubby-holes against the house they can be exciting and stylish, especially if they reflect colours used inside so that again the transition between inside and out is blurred.

When repeated and grouped, key plants become the nuts and bolts that will hold your garden together visually. By repeating plants around a central space, you will create a cohesive feel.

The only way is up

In small gardens there is not always room to bend down and notice the flowers at your feet. Denied the luxury of building our gardens outwards, we have to get upwardly mobile, making full use of vertical space. A good first step designers often use is to lift everything up in raised beds. Using planters mounted onto fences and walls is also a great way of utilising space and can create a vertical tapestry of foliage and form that can be easily seen from the windows of the house.

In her Japanese-inspired design, Fiona George uses window frames filled with vertical 'lawns' of mondo grass, and Peter Bazely made a stunning geometric grid of tillandsias in his minimalist Artists Garden.

THESE PAGES: *Alex Schanzer loves his natives, but he does let in a few outsiders when the need arises. Most often it is bromeliads with their broad, strappy leaves, but here daylilies provide some welcome colour beyond richly textured carpets of swirling* Carex *'Frosted Curls',* Coprosma *'Mangatangi' (centre) and* Muehlenbeckia axillaris *(rear). 'The organic planting shapes are inspired as much by South American designer Roberto Burle Marx as they are by motifs in traditional Maori carving,' explains Alex. 'The negative spaces created by the schist chip are as important as the plants themselves in the design.' Although Alex's wife Rachel did not get to see the plants beforehand, the painting she created on a canvas screen fits perfectly into the restrained colour scheme. With natural materials like the macrocarpa walls and boardwalk and the Bombay bluestone terrace, the result is a very welcoming garden, but to increase the sense of sophistication Alex designed two sculptural light towers at the entrance and reflected them in zinc alume wall panels. The result is a compelling mixture — a design which is stamped with the crispness and worldliness of a modern garden, but is at the same time firmly rooted in an appreciation of New Zealand's unique culture and landscape.*

BOTTOM RIGHT: An elegant courtyard by Serena Blackie, where apparent order and symmetry is made more intriguing by adding 'crooked' details. The window is set to one side and two box topiaries are cleverly staggered to give a formal symmetry if viewed from straight on, but a more intriguing perspective from other angles.

OPPOSITE TOP: Ben Hoyle creates a casual sense of style with recycled materials. Jonathan Campbell designed the oil drum seats, lighting them from inside to showcase the fish-bone cut-outs in the base. The unusual columns clothed in native tecomanthe are made by another artist, Ray Oliver, who glued each layered pebble to the next inside a pipe-mould.

OPPOSITE BELOW: When Richard Greenwood was given his 'junk-yard' challenge — to make a garden from recycled materials — he decided to take the theme as far as it would go. A store security mirror mounted in a car tyre makes a funky focal point. The reflections, coupled with the false perspective of the winding path, increase the sense of depth. The cattle trough planter and sewer pipe sculptures may not smack of high sophistication, but they add a theatrical sense of fun.

FOLLOWING PAGES: Liz Mackmurdie uses her past experience as both a chef and a shepherd to round up the lettuce and lavender, the bean poles and bees, to create this magical potager. (Exhibitor: Big Tree Company)

Focal points and water

When a small-space design is based on symmetry, the eye is led out to a central point or along a path to an end point. Inevitably our eyes expect this kind of focal point as a sort of anchor to hold our attention. Often, garden furniture will form one such sense of focus, but to complement that other points of interest are useful to add a sense of discovery to the garden and to emphasise a theme. Containers, sculptural elements and small water features can all draw the eye and create surprises in different corners.

Sculptures, like pots, need to be used carefully, especially in a confined space. One of the great trends at the Ellerslie Flower Show has been the astronomical rise in interest in garden art. Each year the lake forms the focus for installations of all sizes and textures — rustic carved ponga logs and rusted iron keeping company with sophisticated works in polished steel and stone. It is interesting to note that the classical statuary of years back is moving aside in favour of home-bred designs that strongly reflect our Pacific identity and which blend easily into the contemporary garden.

But no matter how beautiful or expensive, too many focal points can start to turn a tasteful space into something resembling a souvenir shop or a gallery, so some restraint is necessary. The best artworks will reflect and emphasise your chosen theme and mood, and will look comfortable together (rather like a group of relatives as opposed to a motley collection of bystanders waiting at a bus stop).

Water features

The one sculptural focal point many of us cannot resist is a water feature. With the sense of movement, coolness and sound that water brings to a small space, who can resist?

But which water feature? New Zealand style and tastes change so quickly — no sooner had we replaced our ornate Italian fountains with glazed blue water jars than the next fad arrived: water-spurting giant hypertufa balls. The latest trend is for 'chimney pots' of glass, steel and copper — but to keep up with the flow of fashion you will need suitably liquid assets to pay for it all.

The movement and noise of running water certainly add that extra dimension, but it is best to be clear about what sort of animated effects you enjoy. A copper-and-steel creation where the water slides silently down may prove too subtle; at the other extreme, something modelled on the Niagara Falls may get in the way of a quiet conversation.

Fooling the eye

Any device which fights the feeling of claustrophobia in a tight space is to be welcomed. Our eyes are easily fooled when space, distance and perspectives are manipulated by a clever designer.

As in formal gardens, our eyes are instinctively trained to assume that objects appear smaller as they get further away from us and that parallel lines (such as the edges of a path) appear to converge and meet at the horizon. When we break these rules, we can trick ourselves into believing that a space is bigger than it really is.

Reflections are a particularly useful form of visual trickery as they melt boundaries and replicate part of a garden: the simplest might be a still pond lightening a tight space by reflecting the sky. Mirrors are sometimes considered a bit gimmicky, but in small, formal spaces near to the house they can be a useful form of *trompe-l'oeil* or visual illusion, creating the impression of windows into reflected worlds beyond. Mirrors work best when slightly angled and edges are softened with planting.

Today, safer alternatives such as polished steel, aluminium and silvered perspex are more popular, as seen in Green and Grey Spaces (page 85).

Courage and some skill with the paintbrush are needed to pull off a believable mural. Like mirrors, murals need to be blended into the surroundings and are especially appropriate in intimate areas near to the house for pushing out the boundaries with wit and charm.

Meeting the challenge of gardening in a tight space can be rewarding. When you get it right, it is like driving a Mini: what you lack in space, you make up for with style. Inspired choices are required — and events like the Ellerslie Flower Show offer imagination and inspiration. Thankfully, only the boundaries of our gardens need to be limited, not those of our minds.

OPPOSITE TOP: Each of Liz McCloud's three urban courtyards takes on a different colour theme, with the windows providing tantalising glimpses into what lies beyond. Textural stonework, architectural plants and art pieces provide dramatic contrast to the sleek paving and walls, and the shade sail provides a clever visual link between two of the enclosed spaces. (Exhibitor: Kings Plant Barn)

OPPOSITE BOTTOM: By setting the paving at an angle and adding an internal feature wall, Phillipa Deare has broken the box-like feel of this space. The wall supports a sculptural diving board, which can be used as a table or a sun-lounger. Cutting the pavers to fit around the rocks proved to be the most difficult part of the design. (Exhibitor: Garden Design Company)

BELOW: Hedges of Griselinia *and native gossamer grass (*Anemanthele lessoniana*) furnish Sonya Davis' Japanese-inspired cosy yet uncluttered entertaining area.*

Designers and artists appearing in this book include:

Elle Anderson
Tel 09 9688000
see pp 102-103
Sandra Arnet
Tel 09 4109676
see pp 43, 73 (bottom),
130, 131
Mark Atkinson
Enhance Landscapes
Tel 09 8174563
see p 99 (bottom)
Hugo Baynes
Tel 09 3603800
see p 113 (bottom)
Peter Bazeley
Tel 09 5355817
see pp 82 (bottom),
85 (top)
Serena Blackie
Tel 07 8231504
see p 152
Ross Bland
Tel 021 416642
see p 146 (bottom)
Amy Boase
Flower Feva
Tel 09 4384963
see p 46
Clinton Bowyer
Tel 07 5441991
see p 79
Helen Boyes and Lee Cloke
Tel 021 2314567
see p 90 (bottom)
Julie and Brian Boys
Tel 09 4118574
see p 62
Sarah Brill
Tel 09 5352620
see p 70 (top)
Geoff and Liz Brunsden
Wildflower World
Tel 07 5792536
see p 21
Lois Shane Buchanan
Tel 09 4055701
see p 75 (top)
Nigel Cameron
Tel 09 8151719
see pp 43 (top right and
bottom), 48 (right), 49
Michael Cassidy
see p 78
Natalie Clover
Three Gardeners
Tel 025 2090882
see p 146 (bottom)
Peter Collins
see p 45 (bottom)
Phil Cooke
see pp 13 (bottom),

140 (bottom)
Patrick Corfe
Tel 09 3606063
see p 139
Bev Cossar
see pp 13 (bottom),
140 (bottom)
Claudia Daley
Standards of Excellence
Tel 07 5490852
see pp 85, 92
Surendra Dass
Tel 09 3539537
see pp 85, 92,
105 (bottom), 106 (left),
107, 112
Richard Davey
Wairere Nursery
Tel 09 8109699
see pp 113 (top left and
right), 114, 115 (top)
Sonya Davis
Tel 07 8543101
see p 157
Phillipa Deare
see p 156 (bottom)
Mike Denyer
Auckland's Better Gardens
Tel 09 8181183
see p 38 (right)
Wayne Dillon
Tel 09 5799777
Auckland's Better Gardens
see p 142
Kathy Dow
Tel 07 8538422
see pp 19 (bottom),
66 (bottom)
Jamie Durie
Patio Design
Tel 00 61 92803550
see pp 64, 72, 110,
120-121, 123 (top)
David Farley
Tel 09 4128164
see pp 75 (bottom), 108-109
Tim Feather
Tel 09 5289131
see pp 56, 68-69,
70 (top), 145
Fiona George
Japanese Garden Company
Tel 09 4766446
see pp 90 (top), 119
Watson Grayburn
Tel 021 308295
see p 74
Richard Greenwood
Tel 021 674110
see pp 116, 153 (bottom)
Jim Guthrie

see pp 75 (bottom), 108-109
Leslie Harvison
see p 13 (bottom)
Terry Hatch
Joy Plants
Tel 09 2389129
see pp 13 (top), 36-37,
104 (top)
Fiona Henderson
see pp 26-27
Robin Hill
see p 104 (top)
Margaret and Paul Hilton
Waihi Water Lilies
Tel 07 8638267
see p 33 (bottom)
Pamela Howard-Smith
see p 35 (right)
Ben Hoyle
Tel 04 2982034
see pp 32, 119, 153 (top)
Kim Jarrett
Tel 021 430713
see p 78
Leo Jew
Leo Jew Consultants
Tel 021 873668
see p 87, 94
Meg Kane
Tel 09 8207045
see p 67, 87
Jarrod Kilner
see p 67
Virginia King
see pp 44 (top), 78
Jon Lambert
Tel 04 9023481
see p 39
Kate Lang
Tel 027 2776387
see p 69
Norma De Langen
Tel 09 8461083
see pp 88-89
Jan Latham
Tel 027 2730112
see pp 33 (top), 126 (top),
146 (top)
Fiona Lawrenson
Tel 00 44 114 28651776
see pp 22-23
Linda Lee
Pukaki Worm Farm
Tel 09 2759991
see p 61 (top left)
Alison Lennox
Tel 025 441294
see p 9
Sue Linn
Tel 027 6268124
see pp 132-133

Karen Lowther
Tel 09 4160204
see pp 10, 14 (middle),
105, 127, 134 (below),
135
Phillip Luxton
see p 57
Murray Lye
Tel 027 4446025
see pp 24-25, 71, 149 (top)
Kim Macdonald
see p 63 (bottom)
Liz Mackmurdie
Tel 09 8339424
see p 16, 60, 70 (bottom),
123 (bottom), 124, 128
(top left), 154-155
Matt McClean
see p 145
Naomi McCleary
Waitakere City Council
Tel 09 8368000
see p 35
Sally Mcleay
Tel 09 4800916
see p 91
Liz McCloud
Kings
see p 156 (top)
Jane McIntyre
Re:form
Tel 027 4728920
see p 74
Jenny McLeod
Tel 09 8187823
see p 48 (left)
Lisa Mannion
Tel 09 8128143
see p 29 (bottom)
Heather Mark
Three Gardeners
Tel 07 8562570
see p 146 (bottom)
Para Matchitt
Tel 06 8358138
see p 101 (top)
Pamela Matthews
Tel 09 8339049
see p 61 (top right)
Carolyn Melling
Landsendt
Tel 09 8186914
see pp 113 (top left and
right), 114, 115 (top)
Dee Melville-Nel
see p 142
Jack Merlo
Tel 00 61 3 95921700
see p 82
Julena Moors
Tel 09 4129216

Photographic credits

Page 9 Ellerslie Flower Show archives

Page 10 top and middle: Karen Lowther / Ellerslie
Flower Show archives

Page 14 top: Ellerslie Flower Show archives

Page 17 top: Ellerslie Flower Show archives; middle
left and right: Neil Ross

Page 27 right: Neil Ross

Page 29 top right: Ellerslie Flower Show archives

Page 31 top: Neil Ross

Page 33 bottom: Neil Ross

Page 36 top right: Ellerslie Flower Show archives

Page 43 top left: Neil Ross

Page 45 top: Micheal Paul

Page 49 Micheal Paul

Page 50 bottom: Neil Ross

Page 57 Jack Hobbs

Page 59 bottom: Ellerslie Flower Show archives

Page 60 Neil Ross

Page 65 top: Ellerslie Flower Show archives; bottom:
Ellerslie Flower Show archives / Micheal Paul

Page 78 top left and top right: Ellerslie Flower Show
archives / Micheal Paul

Page 82 top left and top right: Micheal Paul

Page 93 Jack Hobbs

Page 99 bottom: Neil Ross

Page 100 left: Ellerslie Flower Show archives

Page 104 bottom: Ellerslie Flower Show archives

Page 105 left: Ellerslie Flower Show archives

Page 106 left: Neil Ross

Page 107 Neil Ross

Page 111 centre left, centre right and bottom:
Ellerslie Flower Show archives

Page 120-121 Neil Ross

Page 122 top left and top right: Ellerslie Flower Show
archives

Page 136 top right: Ellerslie Flower Show archives

Page 143 top and centre left: Neil Ross

Page 148 Neil Ross

Page 149 bottom: Jack Hobbs

Page 156 top left: Jack Hobbs

Page 157 Ellerslie Flower Show archives

New Zealand excellence at the 2004 Chelsea Flower Show. The incredibly popular gold award-winning garden at the Chelsea Flower Show, Ora – Garden of Well-Being, co-designed by Ellerslie Flower Show veterans Trish and Doug Waugh, Lyonel Grant and Kim Jarrett with Tina Hart and Brian Massey. The garden was inspired by the first ASB Discovery Marquee Gondwanaland, see pages 76–78.

This book would not have been possible without the input of countless designers and others involved with the Ellerslie Flower Show, but the biggest thanks must go to my wife, Jose, for keeping me sane, for helping me cut out the waffle and for bearing with me on this project. For their special insight, help and anecdotes, thanks especially to Karen Lowther, Ann Nicholas and Ann Gamble, Jack Hobbs and Berin Spiro as well as Bev McConnell. Thanks also to Renée Lang and Gina Hochstein for their kindness and patience, and to Cath Handley, Chief Executive Officer (Ellerslie Flower Show) for encouraging me to run with the idea in the first place.

Neil Ross